What Others Are Saying about This Book . . .

"Maddie's story is one of generosity, selflessness, vision and hope. Ultimately, it is a reminder, in these jaded times, that doing the right thing still matters, and that we all can make a difference. I had the privilege of forming a friendship with Sharon—and coming to know Maddie's spirit during the filming of a CBC television series, where Maddie's vision was ultimately realized. You can't help but be inspired by their powerful true story."

—**Bruce Kirkby,** *Globe and Mail* **travel columnist,
host of CBC's** *No Opportunity Wasted*

"As a Family Court judge I regularly see parents in conflict who are unable or unwilling to put their children's needs ahead of their own. Maddie's extraordinary story is a heart wrenching reminder that parenthood is a precious privilege that should never be taken for granted. Maddie's life and legacy is a triumph of the human spirit."

—**Justice Harvey Brownstone, Ontario Court of Justice,
Toronto, author of** *Tug of War*

"Maddie Babineau's story is a must read. I was so touched, I wrote a song, 'Move and Be Moved', as a tribute to her extraordinary spirit. We need more people like her in the world!"

—**Brian Melo, recording artist, singer/songwriter,**
Canadian Idol **winner 2007**

"Maddie's spirit lives on in that school, and in the students who will graduate and do great things for their community and their country. In the long term, thousands more children will live because of what Maddie did before she died at fifteen. I'm frequently asked about the most inspiring people I've met, and I've always answered that it's not the politicians, celebrities or business leaders, but the children, like Maddie. You are about to meet the girl who gave her wish away. I know she will change your life, just as she changed mine."

—**Craig Kielburger, co-founder of Free the Children**

"Deep within the heart of this beautiful and courageous child was a wise and benevolent soul. Maddie's story is spellbinding as we live through her pain and suffering while she embraces seeing beyond her-

self and makes sacrifices for humanity with great humility. After you read this incredible true story you will remember a mother's courage and determination to keep her daughter's dreams alive. They say that in every generation there will be someone who will capture our hearts. Both mother and daughter have captured mine. They are true heroes."
—Patricia Karen Gagic, SCA artist, author of *Inspired to be Rewired*, humanitarian "Project Cambodia"

"I base many of my filming decisions on whether or not a story has that "extra-special" something that I call the "goose bump factor." The story of Maddison Babineau, "the girl who gave her wish away," affected me in just that way, inspiring me to tell part of Maddie's story in the *Aim for the Heart—Kenya, No Opportunity Wasted* show, which aired on CBC."
—Morgan Elliott, Emmy-nominated Executive Producer, Suddenly See More Productions, Inc.

"This beautiful and courageous story captures your heart. It inspires you to look within and realize there is so much more to life, and compels you to live it with more meaning."
—Tanya Chernova and Joanna Andros, co-founders of *Courageous Living*, and co-authors of *UnderMIND*

"Much will be written and said when this book is released about the depth of kindness and compassion from a young woman who gave her wish away to help others when she herself was dying. Take Maddie's message into your heart: her selflessness is a model worth emulating."
—Susan McClelland, journalist, author of *Standing Tall*

The girl
who gave
her
wish
away

SHARON BABINEAU

BETTIE YOUNGS BOOKS

Disclaimer: This is a true story, and the characters and events are real. However, in some cases, the names, descriptions, and locations have been changed, and some events have been altered, combined, or condensed for storytelling purposes, but the overall chronology is an accurate depiction of the author's experience.

Cover design by Trevor Shaw and Tatomir Pitariu
Senior Editor: Elisabeth Rinaldi
Photo of Sharon by Alisha Townsend, *Fresh Studios*
Cover Photo of Maddison Babineau by Alisha Townsend, *Fresh Studios*
About the Cover: The photo of Maddison Babineau was taken in 2007, shortly before she passed away.

BETTIE YOUNGS BOOK PUBLISHERS
www.BettieYoungsBooks.com
info@BettieYoungsBooks.com
Bettie Youngs Books are distributed worldwide. If you are unable to order this book from your local bookseller, Espresso, or online, you may order directly from the publisher.
ISBN: 978-1-936332-96-0
ePub: 978-1-936332-97-7

Library of Congress Control Number: 2012911738

1. Babineau, Maddie. 2. Babineau, Sharon. 3. The Children's Wish Foundation. 4. Hope. 5. Children's Health. 6. Cancer. 7. Free the Children Foundation. 8. Healing. 9. Growing Up. 10. Babineau, Maddison. 11. Inspiration. 12. Bettie Youngs Books.

Printed in the United States of America

Dedication

To Maddison (Maddie) Babineau, my guardian angel;
Derek Babineau, my amazing son;
Arunas Antanaitis, my loving husband; and,
Everyone who is courageously making a difference in the world.

CONTENTS

Foreword by Craig Kielburger

I've rarely laughed so hard.

Sitting next to a teenage girl who's suffering chronic pain after multiple surgeries and cancer treatments isn't a scene made for comedy. But Maddie had a way.

From her special bed in front of the living room TV, Maddie introduced me—a *CSI* neophyte—to the complex and hilarious world of the crime-scene investigation drama: the elaborate techniques and lab equipment, the tiny details found thirty-five minutes into the show that wrap the case together, the requisite romantic entanglements. She cracked jokes about the characters, about the plot and about her cancer. She howled when I asked her to explain what had happened at the end of the episode.

With her wicked sense of humor and her utter selflessness, Maddie Babineau made the elephant in the room disappear.

That first meeting with Maddie came shortly after one of the oddest phone calls I'd ever received. It was about a young girl with cancer who was granted a wish—the kind most kids would use for a trip to Disneyland, the latest video game system, or dinner with a movie star. I assumed she might want to go on a volunteer trip to India or Ecuador, or to meet one of Free the Children's inspiring youth speakers she'd heard about.

But this wish, I was told, wasn't *for* the girl. It was *from* the girl. This extraordinary young person, who had lost her father and was fighting for her own life, could have anything she wanted—and she wanted to give to someone who had it worse. She wanted to build a school in Kenya for children in need.

I'm frequently asked about the most inspiring people I've met, and I've always answered that it's not the politicians, celebrities or business leaders, but the children. Like the boy in Salvador, Brazil, who gave me his threadbare shirt—his only possession—as a gift after a game of plastic-bottle soccer. Like the street children who would share a single orange with their entire circle of friends in Thailand. Like Maddie.

That was before I had even gotten to know her and to see how much her whole school loved her, to see her resilience, her remarkable maturity, and her gentle kindness.

I remember visiting her in the hospital and being bombarded with questions about the school she was building a world away, the students and their families, what their community was like. She was so inquisitive, and so committed to making as much of a difference in their lives as she could, which was why she began raising funds on her own to help provide a source of clean drinking water to enhance the impact of their education. She was inspiring.

I feel equally fortunate to have discovered the source of Maddie's strength. Her mother Sharon and brother Derek travelled with us to Kenya shortly after Maddie passed away to help complete the school and water project. They leapt into the grueling physical work, as determined as Maddie was to see it through.

On a day I will never forget, hundreds of people came out to celebrate when Maddie's wish was complete. The full-hearted singing echoed through the valley, and the full-bodied dancing shook the Earth. To the two remaining members of Maddie's immediate family, the community gave a goat—a traditional gift with profound meaning, since most families here could very rarely afford to eat meat.

The most powerful moment happened when the women of the community—the "mamas"—greeted Sharon with warm embraces. In a place where fifty-five babies of every one thousand do not survive past age one, they knew the feeling of losing a child. They held her hands and cried with her, welcoming her as part of their family. It was sad and beautiful all at once, like Maddie's life itself.

As we watched the children run from their new school to the water project Maddie fundraised to build, to see the first trickle of clean water from the new wells, we all felt connected to the girl who made it all possible. Maddie's spirit lives on in that school, and in the students who will graduate and do great things for their community and their country. In the long term, thousands more children will live because of what Maddie did before she died, at fifteen.

And I'll never watch a crime drama without laughing.

You are about to meet the girl who gave her wish away. I know she will change your life, just as she changed mine.

—Craig Kielburger, cofounder Free the Children

A Word from the Author

Imagine a world where wishes come true and love conquers all. That was Maddison (Maddie) Babineau's world, and this is her story.

Maddie was extraordinary in her simplicity and wise beyond her years. These pages are a tribute to the *incredible things* she did. As her mother, I feel a responsibility to bring this message to the world, to share our lessons: about courage, acceptance, celebrating, surviving, giving, and finding peace in the midst of all the trials and challenges of life.

It is a message about hope and the reality that one person can make a huge difference in the world regardless of how old or how young they are.

May it encourage you to live with passion and purpose, and may it also give you comfort and inspiration during your difficult days.

Enjoy this book; share its vision with your family, friends and colleagues. And don't forget: when you are done, close your eyes and make your wish!

With much love and gratitude,
Sharon Babineau, Maddie's mom

Acknowledgements

I have learned that family is everything; let me introduce and thank mine. To my darling daughter Maddie, for choosing (yes, I believe we are chosen) me to be her mom. How she lived and died inspires me to be a better person. To my late husband Stephen, you taught me to live life fully, with no guarantees. To my son Derek, you gave me a reason to carry on. I am so proud of the extraordinary young man you have become. To my husband Arunas, I never believed I could ever love so deeply again, thank you for healing my broken heart, it now pounds wildly because of you. To my parents, Dorothy and Owen, much love and gratitude to you both. To my sisters: Susan, you have carried me during my darkest days, and Angela, your zest for life is contagious. My brothers: Funkle Kevin, for loving Maddie as your own daughter, I am forever grateful. Danny, my amazing big brother. To Stan, my wonderful and supportive stepfather, and Ginny, my stepmother. Thank you all for being in my life.

I have learned that we are stronger as a community; let me introduce my precious friends, colleagues and mentors. My thanks to: Sandi Mousseau, Patricia Cole, Diane LeDonne, Brenda Canning, Patty Cushenan, Judy Cox, Patti Smith Vos, Joanne Sexton, Fran McKechnie, Robin Hahn, Michelle Matuszak, Dekyi Lee Oldershaw, Christine Crawford, Craig Kielburger, Brian Melo, Graeme Newbigging, Tara Stewart, Phil Keoghan, Bruce Kirkby, Morgan Elliott, Maxie Dara Liberman, Lori Golblatt, Vicki Golab, Danielle Scime, Mad4Maddie Committee and Maddie's Everlasting Wish, St. Thomas More High School, St. Jean de Brebeuf High School.

I am grateful for these very special people, who brought this amazing story to life: To my publisher, Bettie Youngs, I am forever grateful for this opportunity. Your trust in my daughter's story has fulfilled my dream of sharing it with the world. Now, we will! Thank you, and thanks to all at *Bettie Youngs Book Publishers* who layered love and expertise to give this book life! To Elisabeth Rinaldi, my editor, who guided my story with respect, sharp eyes and an open heart, you made it better. Bob Spree, for your advice and dedicated attention to detail. Rosanne Leddy, for your medical expertise. Patricia K. Gagic, my warrior sister, who mentored me during my time of doubt and despair, you are a bright light. To Judy Suke, a true book angel and creative force, you sat with me for years on this book, patiently pulling this story out of me. I couldn't have done it without you.

If I missed you, forgive me, know you are always in my heart.

Prologue
An Angel's Message

I stare at the inscription on the gravestone: *Maddison Babineau, "The Girl Who Gave Her Wish Away."* My eyes blur and I look away, *"The Girl Who Gave Her Wish Away"* indeed, "and changed the world while doing so."

I remember how often she said, "Oh Mom, what's all the fuss about? I didn't do much." But, she did. It started with an act of kindness before she died; a simple act of kindness that made the world a better place.

Today we celebrate the first anniversary of her death. We gather together as family, friends, and strangers—connected by our common thread to her.

We grieve over the life of this young girl, taken from us much too soon. Emotions are a combination of heartache and inspiration, sadness and joy.

I stand beside my precious son Derek. I smile as I tightly squeeze his hand; I am thankful for his presence and grateful that he has helped me through this. Only twelve, he is mature beyond his years having witnessed such pain and tragedy. Incredibly, he is my rock and my reason for moving forward every day.

It is unseasonably warm on this cloudless, sunny day. I turn my gaze towards the heavens and watch the hundred orange, red and yellow balloons we had released earlier. They are the color of an African landscape, something that held a special place in Maddie's heart, and although she had never had the opportunity to see it with her own compassionate eyes, her impact on the lives of the children in Africa will never truly be measured. The balloons hovering silently in the thick air, they seem patiently suspended.

Beside me Winston, Maddie's pug, moves and I hear his heavy breathing. I look down and notice how he doesn't object to the pink balloon we have anchored to his tail. As if he understood, he sits in respectful attendance of her.

My eyes are drawn again to the small monument in front of me, covered with flowers, dragonflies, and pictures reflecting her short life. The gravestone reads: "Steven Babineau 1957–1998, and Maddison Babineau 1991–2007."

We had great fun debating a name to suit the gorgeous child who had been given to us. We settled on Maddison, a strong gender-free name that would allow her to do anything she wanted in life. Little did we know that she would live up to her name in such an extraordinary way.

We had buried her with her daddy so they could be together, their brave journeys ending only nine years apart. I imagine that he would have been waiting for her, eager to assume guardianship once again on the day she traded her hospital gown for wings, the same way she looked after him when she was only a little girl. Somehow, that thought brings me comfort.

Just then the wind picks up, and as if moved by an invisible hand, the balloons begin to push forward. Everyone looks up and tracks them as they dance higher and higher. A collective gasp of sheer amazement breaks the silence as the balloons trail a path towards an astonishing vision in the sky.

Two rainbows crossing over each other appear from nowhere and the balloons dot their way toward the gateway formed by these miraculous colorful arches. The balloons dance through the arch, continuing upward. Each balloon represents our love and gratitude for having known such an extraordinary young girl; a girl who changed our way at looking at life.

The rainbows appearing on a cloudless day, as if on demand, seem like a message from Maddie. The rainbows are a gift from her to us. The message from her is clear: "Don't be sad for me. Everything is okay." During her short life she was always looking out for others.

We celebrate as we witness the beauty of "The Magic of Maddie." It was not the first time that we experienced her magic, nor would it be the last.

As I stand at the gravesite, I reflect on the name of the cemetery, "Gate of Heaven." In that moment, with the rainbows overhead, it feels like we are witnessing exactly what the gates of heaven would look like. I whisper a prayer to both of them, releasing my thoughts to join the parade of balloons above.

"Stephen, I love you. Take care of our baby girl."

"Maddie my darling daughter, thank you for choosing me to be your mom; no matter how short the journey. I love you. You were my wish come true, and I could not have asked for a better one."

Prologue

As we leave, the healing process finally begins. The beautiful girl of fifteen, our firstborn, had left behind a legacy that had begun to touch the hearts of nine-year-olds and ninety-year-olds alike.

1

No Guarantees

I have always been a daydreamer. Adventurous and full of curiosity, wanting to one day travel the world. Luckily for me, that fateful spring afternoon, the opportunity presented itself, setting in motion an extraordinary journey of hope, courage and life's greatest lesson.

Running late, as usual, I chased the city bus down the street, banging on the side, alerting the driver to my presence. He pulled over and let me board, it was a good day. A gentleman offered me his seat, I graciously accepted, the day was getting better by the minute. I was exhausted; I closed my eyes, the rocking of the bus lulled me to sleep.

The bus suddenly swerved, waking me from my trance. Looking up, I was drawn to the cute guy standing in front of me, tightly squeezed between a crowd of tired commuters. When the bus unexpectedly braked, jolting him sideways, I saw something even more interesting: a poster ad. In large letters it read, "Join the Canadian military, travel the world, and meet interesting people."

Yes! I thought as I read the poster. *That's it! I'll join the military!* I was young and impulsive; it sounded like a great opportunity to me. I had just graduated from high school, and with my newfound freedom I thought I could do anything, be anything. I had incredible pride in Canada and wanted to help where needed, especially in any peacekeeping work.

"This career sounds perfect for me," I said out loud as I wrote down the contact information, and smiled as I thought of my new future. It was no longer a good day; it was a *great* day!

In April 1979, when I was eighteen years old, I left my hometown of Hamilton, Ontario, to start my adventure with the Canadian Forces. During my career, I traveled across Canada and overseas to Europe where I was posted in Lahr, Germany, at age twenty-two. I was one of the first groups of women vehicle technicians (automotive mechanics) selected for a military trial called the SWINTER (Servicewomen in Non-Traditional Environments and Roles) project.

I had been the only female vehicle technician in my training course back in Canada. I knew this was sure to be an adventure. It was really challenging, physically and emotionally, and yet extremely rewarding. *"There is no life like it."*

Nine years later, when I was posted at the National Defence Medical Centre in Ottawa, Canada, I met Maddie's father, Stephen. It was 1988. He was a civilian, working for Nortel (a communications company). For me, it was love at first sight; however, it took a while longer to win him over. Stephen was three years older than me, had a boyish grin, and looked just like Paul McCartney. He was inquisitive, rode a motorcycle, and loved the outdoors. He had an eclectic taste for food and music. I was swept up in his zest for life and adventure. Life was perfect.

Then, in 1989, he unexpectedly started tripping, and occasionally slurring his words. Once he fell for no apparent reason. When it happened again, we became concerned enough to make a doctor's appointment to find out what was going on. Not expecting anything serious, we were devastated when Stephen was diagnosed with Amyotrophic Lateral Sclerosis (ALS)—a fatal neuromuscular degenerative disease with no known cause or cure. It is better known as Lou Gehrig's disease after the famous New York Yankees baseball player who died of it at the peak of his career. We had never heard of it.

It was a lot to take in all at once. Stephen didn't look or feel really sick, certainly not sick enough to have something as serious as ALS. This must be a mistake, we thought. I held Stephen's hand tightly, secretly willing the doctor to take back those words, that diagnosis, to let us live the life we dreamed of together. But that wasn't the case. Once diagnosed, Stephen was bluntly instructed by the pragmatic doctors to go home and prepare to die.

Die? I thought, stunned by the diagnosis. My eyes filled with tears as I looked at Stephen, struggling to compose myself. He sat there silently; he seemed more poised than I was. He listened intently. I wished I knew what he was thinking.

"You have two, possibly five years at most to live," the doctor said.

But what about our dreams, our future? We had talked about getting married. I turned and asked the doctor, "We want to get married. With this diagnosis, what are our options? Should we still go ahead?"

I don't know why I was asking him this question, as it would really be Stephen's and my choice to make. I was grasping; I just wanted a better understanding of what our future would hold. I wanted some indication of hope from the doctor that others had experienced the same set of circumstances we were facing and lived a rewarding life.

I didn't get the answer I wanted.

"No, not really feasible," the doctor said turning to Stephen. "I recommend you stay at your parents' home, you will need their support in the future."

He looked at me sympathetically, "If you marry, you will be widowed in a few years. You're too young for that. It's a difficult road, I don't recommend it."

The idea of us separating at such a difficult time seemed cruel. I couldn't imagine abandoning him now in his time of crisis. I thanked the doctor and couldn't wait to get away and start planning our future together. I vowed to myself: *We will get through this.*

I hadn't realized how closely Stephen had been listening to the doctor. Caring about me, he seriously considered breaking up. When we got home he said, "Sharon, with this diagnosis, it's just going to be too hard to start a life now. Let's break up. It's the right thing to do."

I knew there were no guarantees in life. I also knew that I was madly in love with Stephen and that I wanted to devote my time, my life, to him. There was no way I would break up. I felt deeply that there must be a reason why we met, something bigger than us, something we weren't aware of yet.

Sitting at the kitchen table, I pleaded, "Let's accept this is going to be difficult, but we can't let the uncertainty stop us. We need to stay together to get through this." Stephen made all his decisions with the greatest consideration and thought. He sat across from me, looking intently, as if he was searching for some sign of sympathy, fear or reluctance in my eyes. All he saw reflected back was hope and love. Finally, he gave in. We decided to move in together. We had no idea of how to cope, and by default started living according to the doctor's predictions. We lived under a dark cloud, as if it was Stephen's last two years.

We were frustrated much of the time. We lacked the skills to deal with the shadow of death and the unknown. We were always worried. What should have been celebrations turned to anxious thoughts: this might be our last Christmas together, this could be our last birthday or anniversary celebration together, this could be our last concert. It left us apprehensive, discouraged, and frightened.

Gradually we came to the realization we could no longer live like that, waiting for the inevitable. It was exhausting; we had had enough of waiting in fear. We were missing out on so much! The truth was Stephen looked great, he was strong. His symptoms were minor: his speech was a bit slurred and he had some weakness in his legs. Our time together was too precious to squander worrying; we needed to save our energy so we could deal with new health issues as they came up.

We decided that Stephen was not *dying* of ALS; he was *living* with ALS. This change of heart, this new perspective, inspired us to live bigger, to make goals regardless of the uncertainty. We began to experience a happier, more satisfying life.

We took a trip of a lifetime, driving to Alaska. We covered over 3,000 miles each way. We explored all the cities and parks and out-of-the-way places. Getting back to nature, being outside, and watching stunning sunsets had a calming effect on us.

We joined a support group when we returned. We started to plan our future and were determined to live life as fully as possible. It was so freeing to feel this way. It was then that we decided that we wanted to have a child. Stephen knew he would live on through his child.

2

Precious Gifts

*L*uckily, once we made that decision, I became pregnant right away. It was as if my body knew that time was not our friend, realizing our urgency to have a baby "now" before it was too late. Finally we could relax. Something positive and "normal" was happening—we were going to have a baby, be a family. We were in control and defying the odds. I was thirty-one years old and thrilled to become a first-time mother. Stephen's joy at becoming a dad was evident. His eyes lit up when I told him. "This baby will be my legacy, the circle of life will be complete," he said enthusiastically.

I savored every moment of the pregnancy, I loved it. In spite of the challenge of working full time and caring for Stephen, I felt fantastic. We excitedly planned for the arrival of the baby and all the changes it would bring into our lives.

During my pregnancy, Stephen's disease advanced, limiting his mobility. He tried hard to keep his independence, but his body defied him. In my eighth month of pregnancy, he had so many problems with his balance and control of his legs, that for safety reasons, he relented and accepted the offer of a wheelchair. It was scary for us how quickly the disease was progressing.

It was a difficult balancing act at times, caring for him while pregnant and not overdoing it. We had to be very careful that neither of us injured ourselves, like the potential to slip and fall when transferring him to his wheelchair, bed or car. We certainly did not want to jeopardize my pregnancy.

I continued to work full time up to the point I gave birth. Physically, it was a very easy pregnancy. Emotionally, it was extremely challenging. Although I tried not to think about it, in the back of my mind was the awareness there were no guarantees that Stephen would even be alive for the birth of our baby.

We were quietly married on August 14, 1991, in the military chapel at the National Defence Medical Centre in Ottawa. Stephen's father, George, had passed away in 1990, not long after Stephen was diagnosed. They were very close, and Stephen was deeply saddened that his father was not around to meet his grandchild.

George had been a pilot in the Canadian Forces. On our wedding day, a large military plane flew over the chapel as we were arriving for the ceremony. As we looked up in awe, it felt like a special fly-pass just for us. We took it as an omen — a sign that we were going to make it just fine.

When I went into labor the following week on August 24, getting Stephen to the hospital was not an easy task. He had to come by Para Transport (wheelchair accessible bus). Stephen's family drove me, and he came separately. He just made it.

The delivery team was fantastic. They quickly saw and understood our situation and accommodated our needs. The nurse was not concerned by Stephen's challenges and gently placed the bundle of joy into his arms as I videotaped their first encounter. The entire room radiated with our joy and excitement.

Stephen was a natural; calm as could be, a proud father, with a great big smile that stretched from ear to ear. It was obvious that this baby was deeply loved and she was a precious gift for us. She was beyond perfect, this little girl with her shocking black hair, bellowing to the world, "I am here!"

I believed she was our miracle baby; if we had listened to the doctors when Stephen was first diagnosed with ALS, we would not have stayed together and she would not have been born. The doctors said Stephen may not live past two years, yet there we were past the dreaded deadline and instead of his death, we had become a family. I could not imagine life without the two of them.

We realized we couldn't make plans for our daughter like other parents. Stephen would not be able to do many things most fathers take for granted. He would not be there for her as she grew up, graduated, got married and had children of her own. This awareness brought urgency to his need to bond with her, and to live fully in the moment.

The two of them would lie in bed together as he whispered to her about his wishes and dreams and desires for her. He would play all his favorite music for her so that she would know and remember a little bit more about him after he was gone.

Stephen, ever the resourceful person, had me buy a Snugly (a cloth, sling-type baby carrier), which we modified so that it attached to him and the wheelchair; then he could carry Maddie as they went for outings together. He proudly drove her around town in his wheel-chair, giving them both a chance to bond as she cuddled into his chest and leaned her head against the beating of his heart.

Maddie was a gentle child. She was loving, shy and had a smile that would light up a room; happy right from the day she was born. I was oblivious to how lucky I was. I wasn't aware of all the problems many first-time mothers have with teething, colic, and sleep-deprivation issues. Maddie was a joy to be with. She seldom cried and went to sleep happy, woke up smiling and stayed much the same way in between; a trait most of us would envy.

I, on the other hand, was a mess of nerves. Blessed to be a mother, blessed to have such a wonderful husband, yet the uncertainly of our future never far from my mind.

As Maddie grew older, it seemed that she was an old soul in a child's body; concerned for everyone she met. She was gentle and soft spoken, her voice almost a whisper; at times you had to lean in to hear her speak. She would look at you with this intensity, as if she was reading you in a motherly way; she was checking to see if you were okay, or needed help.

If she saw someone in a wheelchair she wouldn't shy away, she would march right over and ask them if they needed any help. Then, she would ask them a thousand questions. "Why are you in a wheel-chair?" "How long have you been in your wheelchair?" "Can you walk sometimes?" Not everyone liked her inquisitiveness. I once overheard a woman tell Maddie she was rude for asking so many questions to the young boy in a wheelchair.

Before I could step in and defend her, I heard Maddie say, "My daddy has a wheelchair just like his." Turning to the woman, hands on her hips, Maddie said, "Why am I rude?" Her sincere confusion was enough for the woman to make an excuse and move away.

Maddie never saw her dad as disabled or different. She accepted his wheelchair, his difficulty speaking, all of his struggles. They were never a barrier for her. Even as he struggled and his body betrayed him and he was no longer able to feed himself, she simply and lovingly saw him as Dad. She saw through the limitations the disease put on him. She adored her father.

She also taught others how to accept him and not be afraid. When she wanted to go to the park, he would take her in his big electric wheelchair. She had realized that her friends were afraid of him in that thing. One day she came to me with a great idea. She stood there in her pink top, blue jeans and a hat that looked like a conductor's hat. "Mom, can you help me?" she said. "I want to connect my wagon to Dad's wheelchair."

"Why, Maddie, do you have something to bring to the park? If so I can carry it for you instead."

"No. I want daddy's wheelchair to pull my wagon," she explained.

"Are you tired?" I asked.

Exasperated, she said, "No, Mom, I want my friends to come to the park and play with daddy and me."

"I still don't get it Maddie, why do we have to hook up the wagon to your dad's wheelchair?"

"Because it would be fun, silly!" she said. "Dad can give us free rides, like a choo-choo train!"

With the technical help from her engineering dad, the two of them designed a way to hook up Maddie's little red wagon with a bungee cord to the back of the wheelchair. Her wagon, or as she called it "choo-choo train," would hold two people comfortably, maybe three if they squished tightly together.

She went down the street with her dad and knocked on a friend's door. "Come out and join me for a ride," she said. Then off to another friend's house. "Come for a train ride to the park," she announced. They would come out all excited and jump on board.

As they rolled away, I walked a few paces behind, in awe of what Maddie had just done. Her delight in life, her ability to find fun under any circumstance, amazed me. Her friends were no longer apprehensive around Stephen. He didn't seem as scary in his big wheelchair anymore. They were just having fun.

In 1994, Maddie and her dad were featured on the Muscular Dystrophy Labor Day Telethon, to raise awareness for ALS and to show others how our family coped. The cost of caring for someone with ALS could easily bankrupt a family. We were lucky we had medical insurance through each of our employers; we learned many other families struggled. We were adamant to raise awareness and funds for such a devastating disease.

Maddie, always a giving spirit, raided her piggybank to support the MD Telethon. It was her first act of philanthropy at the tender age of three. The camera captured her with her little blue-and-white striped top and leggings, standing on her tip toes, pouring the change into a large glass container. This unselfish act was a prelude to what would come. I still have a certificate of appreciation from the organization with her picture and her name on it proudly hanging on our wall.

As Stephen's illness progressed, Maddie became even more attentive. She would care for her dad and make him laugh. I'll always cherish the memory of the day I came home from work and found her sitting on Stephen's lap. There was an empty box of Kleenex on the table. Beside him, and all around him, the floor and chairs were covered with little crunched up balls of tissue. Thankfully, I didn't see any blood. I wasn't sure what had taken place and when I asked Stephen, he smiled and nodded towards Maddie.

"Maddie what happened?" I asked, concerned something might be wrong.

She looked at me with a serious look, as intent as a four-year-old can get, her brow was furled and she said with the most indignant tone: "Mom, Dad had a 'booger' in his nose and I just couldn't get it out."

I realized she had been torturing him while I was away. All with good intentions, of course, and poor Stephen hadn't the strength or desire to stop her as she drilled up his nose—almost to his brain—delicately performing "booger" surgery. She was such an intense kid. That situation would have grossed almost anyone out, but not her, she was saving her dad from the annoying booger!

That year, Stephen's condition continued to worsen, and he needed additional medical care. Daily help with toileting, getting him up each morning and putting him to bed at the end of the day was arranged through the Community Care Access Centre. It was only two hours of help a day, but it made all the difference in the world.

Despite Stephen's weakening condition, we talked about having another child. We both thought it would be wonderful for Maddie to have a brother or sister to play and grow up with. I had always wanted more than one child. Stephen and I both came from large families. I was one of five children and always loved the energy of a full-house of kids.

Aware that we were living on borrowed time, we put our trust in the unknown and followed our hearts. One year later, on December 15, 1995, we were blessed again –this time with a beautiful son, Derek. He too was an absolute joy.

We had a perfect family. Stephen had his legacy, two precious gifts: Maddie and Derek.

3

Maddie, the Little Mother

Derek was a more active baby than Maddie. Maybe it was because it was my second pregnancy and I knew what to expect, but I was more relaxed. I even continued running during my pregnancy; it was a great stress reducer and I was glad the doctor said I didn't have to give it up. Derek was always on the go, and I joked that it was a result of all the bouncing he experienced in my belly when I was jogging.

Maddie adored her brother and fussed over him as if he was her favorite doll. Now, she had two people to look after: her dad and Derek. At four and a half, she was more helpful and caring than other children her age. She never complained when I called her away from the TV, even while watching her favorite purple dinosaur, Barney. She took great pleasure in retrieving anything for her dad and especially Derek.

She took delight in using her early maternal skills by learning how to feed them both: her dad in a wheelchair and her little baby brother in his kiddy seat. Of course to watch this was hilarious as each mouthful bypassed the mouth and landed anywhere else. With a determined look on her face, her eyes squinted up, and her mouth open mimicking what she wanted them to do, she worked away with determination and great patience.

Maddie would help Stephen get around by climbing on his lap and driving his wheelchair for him. She would laugh and giggle as she sped through the house. She learned to corner easily and park effortlessly. Of course there were a few dings in the wall; admittedly most of them from me. I imagined her at eighteen, squealing into the driveway in a bright red Ferrari.

Often, Maddie would sit with her dad as he read the Saturday paper and would patiently wait for a sign from him to turn the pages. Sometimes she pretended she could read, making up elaborate stories for Stephen and Derek. Maddie was conscientious, too, stacking away toys that her little brother left out so that there was a clear path on the floor for Stephen to maneuver his wheelchair. She acted as if it was an honor for her to care for him. You could see she felt needed and she had fun doing it; she was a little mini-mom.

Maddie was shy, but made friends very easily. I think it was her transparent innocence and sincerity that children were attracted to. She simply shined. She enjoyed everything—going to her daycare, her school, and spending time at home with us. She also had a daring side: she loved roller coasters and waterslides; for her, the faster or higher the better. The daredevil streak was absolutely inherited from her dad, and Stephen loved encouraging her!

Maddie had a best friend named Jeremy. He was a young boy her age who lived a few houses down the street. His mother Christine and I were also good friends and we often would take the kids to the park or movies as we discovered the beauty of living in Ottawa. The kids loved to be outdoors and were inseparable.

One Valentine's Day, there was a knock at the front door, and it was Jeremy. He gave Maddie her first bouquet of red roses and probably her first heartfelt blush along with them. Not bad for a five year old! Jeremy had set the bar high and I pitied any future boyfriend who dared to show up empty-handed on Valentine's Day in the future.

Stephen's disease continued to ravage his body and he became weaker and needed more care. With limited homecare, and very little outside support, Stephen spent long hours alone during the day. On one occasion this proved to be like a surreal scene out of a movie. I was at work and the children were at daycare.

Stephen was in his bedroom gazing out the window when our home was broken into. A burglar came in through the back door. Stephen saw him, but was unable to dial 911 as he had no use of his arms or voice. All he could do was pray the robber did not come through the apartment and see him in his bedroom. Luckily, the thief did not discover him. He rummaged through items in the living room; stole the video camera and a few other things before fleeing as quickly as he came.

The "stuff" that was taken could be replaced. What was really stolen that day was our peace of mind and sense of security. It was then we realized how truly dangerous and vulnerable our situation was. While I was away at work Stephen's exposure was completely unacceptable. His inability to defend himself raised really tough questions. "What if there was a next time? What if there was a fire?" "Would help find him in time?"

This was a cold slap in the face for us, a wake-up call, to realize how fragile our lives had become. I broke down and wept as I worried about our future. "How can we make this work?" It seemed impossible.

We struggled to manage our circumstances and we were now facing the hard truth, things had to change. We had talked about a long-term care facility right at the beginning of his illness, and we agreed that was never to be an option. I was afraid, if Stephen was admitted to a long-term care hospital, he might give up on life. He was the head of our household and not only did he need a purpose to continue living, we, his children and wife, also needed him. We were a family.

There were few options left and the only logical one was for me to quit my job. The thought of leaving my career was devastating. I had served over nineteen years in the military. It was all I knew. I was a proud Canadian soldier, but realized defending and serving my family had to come first. I handed in my release papers and requested an early retirement from the Canadian Forces. It was granted immediately.

With Stephen on disability from his work, and I no longer employed in Ottawa, we decided moving back to my hometown of Hamilton, Ontario, might better serve our situation. There we would have some support from my family and friends that we needed so badly.

Getting back to Hamilton presented a myriad of complex problems that we had not anticipated. The first issue was wheelchair accessibility. We could not find a suitable home that would accommodate Stephen and his chair; the only option was to build our own home.

As luck would have it, during one of my house-hunting trips my real estate agent found a contractor with a ready-to-build-on parcel of land that would suit our needs perfectly! By April of the following year (1998) our home was ready. All of Stephen's needs would be met. The home had a walk-out basement giving him access and freedom to the outdoors that he so loved.

It seemed that there was no shortage of obstacles. As quickly as I would dart away from one, another would show up. Upon moving to a new city we had to find a doctor who would be willing to take Stephen on as a patient and would consider making house calls. We also waited patiently for the delivery of a hospital bed. It seemed we were constantly modifying the house as Stephen's needs increased.

On May 17, only six weeks after moving back to Hamilton, tragedy struck. I went in to wake Stephen up for breakfast. As I gently touched him I realized he was not breathing. I tried frantically to resuscitate him for what seemed like forever, but he was not responding.

I reached for the phone beside the bed and dialed 911. The voice on the other end was calm and soothing. I, however, was in a panic, "My husband's not breathing!" The voice continued to calmly guide me.

Within minutes our home was surrounded by a fire truck, two ambulances and a police car. Thank goodness our neighbors were so compassionate; they quickly ushered Maddie and Derek to their home so that I did not have to worry about them.

At the hospital, the doctors confirmed that Stephen had passed away peacefully during the night. They brought me to the small room that held his body and I was given all the time I needed to say good-bye. I held him for what seemed like hours and then a soft voice and gentle hand guided me out of the room. I was beyond heartbroken knowing it was the last time I would ever see my loving husband.

Walking out the hospital doors my mind raced as I remembered our journey together. We laughed, cried, dreamed, survived and we always believed in each other. Now, I would be filling in for two parents and carrying the future on my shoulders. I was barely able to contain myself as I looked up into the sky and whispered, "Stephen, guide me." I prayed this over and over as I steadied myself to tell our children their daddy had died.

I really believe in my heart that Stephen held on, waiting for our house to be built. He knew how important it was for me to move closer to my mother and siblings. The day before he died, he was sitting by the window watching his children play in the front yard. He had found his inner peace knowing that we would have a better life, and that we were happy. I believe Stephen felt he no longer had to suffer.

Maddie was only six, and Derek was two years old when their father died. I worried, thinking, *How do you explain death to young children?* When I came home from the hospital, I sat them down and told them, "Daddy's gone to heaven." Maddie cried, Derek looked at her and began to cry, too. I don't think he understood what it meant, but if his big sister was crying, then he felt he needed to cry, too.

Maddie was deeply saddened and anxious; being older she understood her daddy would never come home, but Derek would ask day after day, "When is daddy coming home?" I never knew how to respond.

They missed him so, it was confusing and scary and heartbreaking for them. Maddie was quiet and accepting as if she had known that it was coming.

Stephen's courageous journey ended nine years after he was given his two-year prognosis. Our miracle was in living and valuing every single moment without anyone else's rule book. We had earned our Ph.D. in life. The doors that we walked through became the training ground for what was to follow. Stephen left me understanding the depth by which we must live our lives. He was our hero.

We were now a family of three who, together, would move on and be his legacy.

4

What's Wrong with Me?

After Stephen's death, I began working full time again. Although I had my military pension, it wasn't enough to raise a family on. I accepted a job as an auditor in a casino in Milton, just over an hour away. The commute was long—especially during the winter months. I was working evenings and some weekends, and the shift work was difficult on all of us. Not only were Maddie and Derek dealing with the loss of their father, but also my new work obligations.

Although she had her own insecurities, just like we all do at that age, I thought Maddie was handling things well. When she was eight, I signed her up for some art classes and swimming lessons at the local community center. She would attend the art class first, and then walk down the hall to swim classes, where she would be joined in the pool by her brother. The first day, I walked her to her art classroom and I asked her if she was comfortable going in on her own. I told her it would help me out, and she agreed. Each week I would drop her off, then Derek, and I would meet up with her an hour, later.

This went on for three weeks. Each week after class, I asked her how her art lessons were going. "Fine," she would always say. When I asked to see her drawings, she would never show them to me, saying, "Mom, they're mine. It's private." One day when she had put down her portfolio to change into her swimsuit, I picked it up. I couldn't wait to see what she had been drawing.

When I opened her book, I was shocked to see that it was blank. Nothing on the first page. I turned it over, nothing on the second page. I started flipping through, all the pages were blank. Confused, I sat Maddie down and asked for an explanation. "Maddie, have you been going to art class?" I asked.

"No," she said, staring at the changing room floor.

"Why not?" My heart skipped a beat as I realized Maddie was hiding something from me.

"Because they're all better at drawing than me!" she blurted out, seemingly relieved to have been finally caught.

"If you haven't been going to art class, then where have you been going?"

"I stay in here," she said, waving her arms around the changing room. "I sit and wait till swim class starts."

She looked away and started to fiddle with her gym bag.

"Maddie, you never have to hide something from me. Next time, tell me what's wrong, and we can find a solution." I was worried by her actions. I realized that she had anxiety—believing she wasn't good enough for the group. The other people in the class were older, teenagers and adults, and I think that intimidated her.

I tried to talk her into returning to the class. She was adamant about not going, unwavering in her stance that she did not fit in. This was the first sign of a stubborn streak I would witness in her. I wasn't sure how to handle it, so I thought it was best to just let it go.

I remember thinking, *The world sometimes devours the weak; if this keeps up, what will happen to Maddie?* I had no idea at the time of the irony of that thought, and how such a wonderful child would prove me wrong.

The long commute and shift-work schedule eventually proved too taxing, so I decided to seek a job closer to home. The Halton Regional Police Service was advertising for a civilian position as an alarm coordinator and Crime Stoppers support person. I thought it sounded like a unique change and jumped at the chance to apply. Fortunately, they hired me and I stayed with them for three years.

During that time I continued my personal commitment of volunteering for the ALS Society of Ontario. Eventually I became the chapter president. The governing board felt that the growth in the community warranted opening a Regional Office in Hamilton and the job of regional manager was offered to me.

It was equally exciting and scary to move from a job with a wonderful future, benefits and good friends, to this new career. I was nervous as the pay was less, there was no pension plan or guarantee the office would be a success. Yet, I knew how hard it was to cope with ALS. My compassion for families and my personal experience and understanding of the disease would be a great fit. Who would be a better suited for this role than someone who has already walked in their shoes? My experience with Stephen and his illness had taught me that we must take risks if we want to live fully. I made the switch.

Maddie and Derek quite often attended the support group meetings I facilitated, just like the support groups we had attended when Stephen was alive. Maddie's ability to warm the hearts of everyone there never ceased to amaze me. She was always engaging, chatting easily with the patients. She had a special way of communicating and had charm beyond her years. She was both curious and caring. At such a young age, she already had a unique understanding of people's struggles.

Some patients were in wheelchairs, some had great difficulty speaking, and some used computer-generated voice synthesizers. Maddie would patiently wait to hear what they had to say and then could hardly wait to share one of her own silly made-up stories. She loved to make people laugh. Maddie's eyes danced as she engaged in dialogue with the groups. Her smile radiated from the inside out. When I reflect back, it was almost as if she was meant to be by my side, easing people's suffering with her deep but innocent wisdom.

When patients died, Maddie and Derek would often accompany me to the local funeral parlor as I paid my respects to the families. I was very committed and never quite thought of it as a job but rather an honor to support them.

The more time she spent time with the grieving families and patients, Maddie began to showing great strength. She realized that one person's actions can make a world of difference to others. Little did we know how this would become the training ground for her own battles.

* * *

When she was eleven years old, Maddie started complaining about a pain in her back. "It hurts and sometimes wakes me up." she would say. Sometimes it was just a fleeting pain. Other times it bothered her to the point where she couldn't get comfortable enough for a good night's sleep. In fact, it seemed to be worst at night, when she was lying down trying to rest.

Thus began the many trips to our family doctor. Maddie's symptoms were vague. The doctor would poke around her back and test her arms' range of motion, trying to find anything conclusive. He suggested that perhaps it was growing pains.

Maddie complained that her mattress was lumpy and uncomfortable. I replaced it, but her discomfort continued. She asked if she could sleep with me and, naturally, I let her.

Her pain continued, and eventually got worse. We returned to the doctor and he recommended physiotherapy, which she attended for months. The office was around the corner from our home and we would walk over together after school. They set up a series of exercises designed to strengthen her arm. At one point during the treatment, they taped up her shoulder to help straighten it, in an attempt to realign her back.

The physiotherapy didn't seem to offer any her relief, and although the pain was intermittent it was persistent. After twelve months of this pain, Maddie came to me one day and said, "Mommy, when I do this, I don't feel anything." She scratched along her left arm repeatedly, showing again how she felt no sensation. It sounded unusual, but I wasn't too alarmed. We went back to the doctor and this time he ordered an X-ray of Maddie's spine. He thought perhaps she had scoliosis, a curvature of the spine. Depending on the severity it doesn't always require treatment. It was a relief to see that tests were being scheduled to further investigate what the cause of the pain might be.

When we went to the medical center for the X-rays, we joked around while waiting in the reception room. Maddie happily chatted about her upcoming overnight seventh-grade trip to Camp Brebeuf. She got the X-rays, and they sent us on our way.

We returned home, and the X-rays were forgotten as we had something much more fun to think about. Maddie was very excited and looking forward to the adventures that lay ahead on her class trip. We packed her bags, and I drove her to her school. I watched all the kids, giddy with excitement, getting on the bus. Maddie turned to me, smiled her magnificent smile and waved good-bye. I blew her a kiss and watched the bus drive away until it was out of sight.

The next day, I wasn't feeling well. I called our doctor and made an appointment to see him in the afternoon. As the morning passed, I started to feel better and decided I could make it through the day. I had a very full work schedule and really needed to get to the office, so I called the doctor back to cancel my appointment.

The receptionist responded, "Wait. Don't cancel! You of all people need to come in today. Hold on, please, the doctor needs to speak to you." The doctor came on the line and in a grave voice said, "I have to see you today, it's important."

At first, I didn't understand, and then I remembered Maddie's X-rays. The results must have come back. I felt a chill run down my spine and started shaking. "It's about Maddie, isn't it?"

"Yes," he replied, "I'm very sorry, it's not good news."

It was a beautiful, sunny June day. I was outside on the front lawn. The warmth of the sun seemed to fade as I absorbed the impact of the doctor's words. I dropped to my knees, the phone still in my hand. I couldn't breathe. I couldn't believe there was something wrong with my daughter.

I thought, "Dear God, not again—not my little girl." My mind overflowed with the same horror I had experienced when we lost Stephen. I couldn't think straight. I knew I couldn't drive safely. Sobbing, I called my older sister, Susan. She rushed over and drove me to the doctor's office.

Our doctor explained that the X-ray showed a massive tumor. Maddie needed further testing. It didn't look good. His tone was alarmingly severe. I collapsed in my sister's arms, grateful she was there with me to help me absorb the shocking news.

The next day I went to Maddie's school. I talked with the principal, trying to decide whether or not to bring Maddie back from camp early. The principal called the camp and they told her that Maddie was okay and having a fabulous time. With that reassurance, I decided that she would be fine and probably needed the time away. I thought about Stephen and how important these rare and beautiful moments were in everyone's life. I had to let it be.

It was just as well that she was away. I needed the two days to process all of this.

I met her bus and watched her walk down the aisle as she made her way out. She looked quite pale and unwell. I was extremely relieved to see her and I held her tightly. I noticed that she felt very hot. She immediately complained about her arm hurting. I took her home and put her to bed.

I had picked up the X-rays earlier that day, and our family doctor told me he was booking an appointment with a specialist. I took the film over to my neighbor, who was a nurse and a good friend. In light of the fact that Maddie had a fever, she suggested we bundle her up and take her to the hospital emergency room.

I knew Maddie was really sick when she didn't complain about my fussing over her to go to the hospital. She was admitted the minute we got there.

It was the beginning of the lengthy process of trying to diagnose the tumor and whether it was benign or malignant. Maddie looked extremely unwell, she was running a fever and was withdrawn. My bubbly, charming Maddie was unable to hide her pain. Reluctantly she followed the doctor's instructions, enduring the poking and prodding as they ran blood tests and more X-rays.

The staff admitted Maddie as an in-patient on 3B of the Children's Ward. This is where she would stay while the doctors continued their investigation into her illness. As we exited the elevator, we were assaulted by the sounds on the ward: children crying, machines whirling, and bells going off all around us. The nurse pushed Maddie in a wheelchair down the hall to a hospital bed. Maddie was tired from the pain medication she had been given. I could barely see her snuggled under all the blankets. Her small face showed the exhaustion of the ordeal as she drifted in and out of sleep.

They soon assigned Maddie a room where a fold-out chair would become my bed during her stay. While she slept, a nurse gave me a quick tour of the ward, pointing out where the showers and kitchen facilities were located.

I made a quick phone call home to check on Derek. My brother, Kevin, had rushed to the house to care for him when we had left for the hospital. Kevin said that Derek was sleeping. "Tell him I love him and that we'll be home soon," I said, wishing I could be in two places at once.

5

Devastating Diagnosis

On June 17, 2004, we were ushered into a small, white sterile room at McMaster Children's Hospital. The nurse placed Maddie's file in the holder on the door and left us. Maddie, my brother, Kevin, and I, anxiously sat waiting for the doctor to arrive. I tried to think of what we could possibly talk about—thinking any small talk would do.

Before I could start a mindless conversation, the doctor walked into the room and sat down in front of us. He started to talk, but strangely the words he uttered made no sound. His lips moved but I heard nothing. I wondered if I was sleeping and in a dream. I finally realized that he was telling us they had found a large tumor in Maddie's chest. She was diagnosed with Ewing's sarcoma, a rare and aggressive form of bone cancer.

Maddie looked so tiny, sitting on the examination table, her legs were swinging back and forth while the doctor and I discussed her diagnosis and treatment. I tried to stay calm, but I was screaming on the inside. I watched Maddie out of the corner of my eye as the doctor explained everything; it was a lot to take in.

My daughter never said a word; she barely looked up at us the whole time. Her light blue hospital pajamas were at least two sizes too big. She picked at a loose thread on her pants, concentrating on unraveling it. The thread required her attention; it needed to be unraveled, allowing Maddie to temporarily escape from what she may or may not have heard and understood.

Cancer! How could that be? She wasn't even old enough to smoke or have any bad habits. She had barely lived. How could a twelve-year-old child have cancer?

The pediatric oncologist, a doctor who specializes in treating children with cancer, explained Maddie's proposed treatment: one whole year of chemotherapy, followed by surgery and radiation. This was the universal protocol, meaning it was the standard treatment for this disease around the world. Although it was a standard treatment, the oncologist also wanted her to be part of a special clinical trial for further development in the study and treatment of Ewing's sarcoma.

The protocol listed all the potential side effects and complications: nausea, vomiting, heart arrhythmias, hair loss, sores, pain, and many more long-term effects. The list was quite alarming, with page after page of frightening information. I hesitated and reluctantly signed the authorization to allow Maddie to participate in this trial. I had to believe that it would save her.

I needed to get her out of the room. I could see that Maddie was becoming anxious, and I was worried that we were scaring her. I knew that there were going to be many more questions to answer and meetings to attend. For now, Maddie needed to rest. I simply wanted to get her back to her room and settle her down.

"Let's go Maddie," I said softly as I wrapped my arms around her and guided her to her room. "Would you like to rest for now?" I asked, sensing she did not want to talk about her diagnosis yet.

"Yes, Mom, later okay?" she said, smiling weakly. I tucked her into her bed, and kissed her forehead. I wanted to hold her tight and tell her everything would be fine. I wasn't even sure she comprehended what had just happened.

"Let's talk tomorrow okay?" I said. She didn't answer; she turned on her side and closed her eyes.

I walked through the hospital doors and sat down on a bench outside the entrance. A tsunami of pain overwhelmed me. I visualized my beautiful Maddie, lying upstairs in that hospital bed without me. There are no words to describe this moment. As frightened as I was, I realized that my warrior heart needed to kick in. I told myself, *Everything will be okay, everything will be resolved. Maddie will fight this. We will fight this together.* I had to believe my own words. And then I began to think about Derek—I needed to be there for him. I needed to make sure that he would understand what was happening. I had to make a plan.

I talked with Kevin. I worried about the instability of moving Derek between relatives—grandparents, uncles, and aunts. We decided it would be best for Derek to stay at home, and Kevin would live at our house. He had already become a father figure to both the kids since Stephen's death. They had nicknamed him Funcle Kevin, a combination of father and uncle. I trusted that this was the best solution: knowing Derek would be lovingly cared for and allowing me to concentrate on being there for Maddie.

The next day, I knew I had to talk to Maddie about her cancer diagnosis. I needed to know what she understood. I had to develop an approach that would not frighten her, but would help her understand and feel safe. I really wanted her to open up to me and share her feelings so that our conversations about the process, the treatment, and moving forward would be easier on both of us.

In the morning after breakfast, I sat on her bed and wrapped my arms around her. "Remember when Uncle Kevin was diagnosed with cancer?"

"Yes," she quietly replied.

"And he got better, right?" I confidently told her.

"Yes," she nodded in agreement.

"And then Nanny got cancer."

Again, "Yes, I remember," she said.

"What happened to her?" I asked.

"She got better," Maddie answered. I felt her demeanor change. She sat up straighter.

I kept building my case for success. I made the argument, "They were fighters, right?"

"Yes," she said with confidence.

Looking her in the eye, I demanded, "And I know you are a fighter. Right?"

"I guess . . ." she replied with some hesitation in her voice.

"You are the strongest fighter I have ever met," I said, hugging her tightly. "I know you can get through this. We will get through this together."

I turned and looked directly into her eyes again, "I promise I won't leave your side. You will never be alone."

"Okay, Mom." She returned my hug just as fiercely.

She wasn't saying much, and I wished I could read her mind. I knew she had a lot to take in, and I realized that maybe I needed to give her time to process it all. We would have to talk more about this later.

We sat holding each other for a very long time, both of us unsure of what was to come, yet somehow we knew we would face each day together.

6

Evil Kool-Aid in a Bag

Maddie spent the week following her diagnosis preparing for her first chemotherapy treatment. She underwent a minor surgery to get a Port-a-Cath (PICC) put in her chest. It is a small medical appliance that is inserted just beneath the skin. The port allows the medical staff to inject drugs and draw blood samples so the patient does not require repeated, painful needle pokes.

We quickly learned the ins and outs for the protocol she was undergoing, including CT scans, PET scans, MRI's, X-rays, bone scans, echocardiograms, neupogen injections and blood transfusions; most of it was completely foreign to us.

Despite the years spent with Stephen's declining health, and being familiar with hospitals and sickness, nothing had prepared us for this new world of cancer. Much of Stephen's treatment had consisted mostly of home care and nursing. He had an occasional X-ray or blood work, but nothing as complex as what Maddie would be going through.

All the tests booked were an indication that Maddie's illness was very serious. Lots of diagnostic tests were needed to determine the location and size of the tumor and to ensure it had not metastasized in other parts of her body.

She had a bone scan, which involved injecting radioactive material (radiotracer) into her blood system. A special camera takes pictures of how much radiotracer collects in the bones. The camera moves from above and around the sides of the patient's body. It takes about an hour. Maddie found it difficult to lie still on the hard table for that length of time.

A CAT scan was ordered. It is an X-ray procedure that shows three-dimensional images of the internal organs and structures of the body. Maddie went into what looked like a large donut-shaped X-ray machine, the table moved right through the hole. She was not able to move during the testing. At least this one took only twenty minutes.

I stood nearby, covered in protective garments, watching her bravely endure the procedure.

After three days, she started to get a bit antsy about all the tests. Finally, her last test came on the fourth day: an MRI. The MRI uses a magnetic field and radio waves to create detailed images of the patient's body. This machine makes some people feel claustrophobic. The patient is strapped in and caged so that they can't move, then the patient slides into the machine and stops, encased completely in the metal tube. Loudly, the mechanisms move around them. When Maddie was asked if she wanted to be sedated for the test, she declined; she said she wasn't scared. Maddie's procedure took about thirty minutes, and she had only the headphones with music to protect her from the extremely loud noise of the magnets.

We got the results. The cancer had not metastasized. This was good news. It renewed our belief that Maddie was going to beat her cancer. The doctors prepared her preliminary treatment schedule: her chemo would start the end of June, and be completed the following May in 2005. Surgery would be considered after a few rounds of chemotherapy. If her body responded to the drugs, and the tumor reduced in size, they would consider removing the residual tumor by surgical intervention. This would be in a few months, around October. The chemotherapy would restart after her surgery.

We quickly got into a routine: breakfast at 8:00 A.M., medical rounds by the doctors at 10 A.M., then, if there were no tests scheduled, Maddie was free to do what she wanted for the rest of the day. The nurses encouraged her to eat lots of food, and get up and walk around; this was to keep up her strength and muscle tone. Her chemotherapy would be starting in a few days.

We decided that since Maddie was going to be spending so much time there, we needed to personalize her environment, her room and the ward kitchenette. Maddie wrote "BABINEAU" on a piece of sticky paper and put it on our designated shelf so there wouldn't be any confusion. Then she made another one, and wrote "MADDIE" on it, claiming a small corner of the shelf for herself. "For my chips and chocolate bars. I can't be expected to eat only hospital food," she said, rolling her eyes.

In her room, Maddie painted a red poster with her name on it and taped it on the outside of her door. It read "Maddie's Room" and was decorated with hearts. "In case anyone is coming to visit me, this will help them find me," she said.

My bed, the fold-out chair, was situated in the corner of her room. It wasn't very comfortable; my legs stuck out and interfered with staff members as they entered and exited the room. We hadn't been sleeping well during the night; it was very difficult to get used to all the crying children and ringing bells. Tired, I had fallen asleep in the middle of the afternoon, so deep in sleep that I started to snore.

"Mom, behave, I have a roommate now!" Maddie pleaded.

I quickly sat up. She looked at me with a look that only Maddie could give. Her head cocked to the right side, her right eyebrow slightly raised, a look of bemusement, or disbelief (I never knew which) and the corner of her mouth lifted revealing a semblance of a half-smile. It was a look I had seen many times before, and one you don't want to mess with.

"Sorry, Maddie," I said, as I quickly sat up and turned towards her new roommate. The young girl had arrived an hour earlier. She had been coming into the hospital for different medical treatments, something to do with her lungs. She seemed to know her way around and was encouraging Maddie to go and make crafts with her.

"Melissa—Mom." "Mom—Melissa," Maddie said, quickly getting the formalities over with. "Melissa knows how to make stained glass, we are going to get some craft supplies and make some window catchers. See you later!" She jumped out of bed, and off they went.

An hour later, the doctor entered the room, holding Maddie's medical file. I asked him to wait while I went to get Maddie. When she came back to her room, her smile had been replaced with a look of apprehension. She sat on her bed puffing up her pillow, as if it was the most important thing she could be doing. The nurse who was on rounds with the doctor pulled the curtain around Maddie's hospital bed, giving us the illusion of privacy; although others couldn't see anything, they could still hear everything that was said.

The doctor smiled at Maddie, "Well young lady, your treatment will start tomorrow. Expect to be here for a week and we will try to get you back home on the weekend. You can start your summer holidays at home."

The idea of going home in a week was welcoming. When she was diagnosed, Maddie had just two weeks left of grade seven. All her school tests were finished so she did not have to worry about making up any work; she could relax and enjoy the summer.

The next day we woke up to the duty nurse bringing in Maddie's breakfast. "Sit up Maddie and eat, your chemotherapy will start later today. It's good to get some food into your stomach first."

In front of Maddie was a bowl of cereal, dry toast and some apple-sauce. Not too inviting.

"Maddie, do you want to go to the cafeteria and get some real food?" I asked, thinking that this might be the last normal meal she would have for some time. We had been warned she might get sick and nauseous from the chemotherapy drugs.

"Yes," she enthusiastically replied, "let's go before they come back to take me."

We were informed she was going to have an IV inserted later in the morning. Maddie wanted to avoid being poked as long as possible. She put the lid back on her plate and pushed the tray away and slipped out of bed. We walked down the hall in silence, both lost in thought about the upcoming treatment.

When we returned, the nurse was waiting for Maddie in the room. "Time to hook you up, sweetie," she said.

Maddie rolled up her sleeve and extended her slender arm. "I'm going to start with an intravenous and give you some fluids. Then, later today, we will be starting your chemotherapy. Okay?"

Maddie looked at her bravely. "Okay."

At 2:00 P.M., the nurse returned, carrying a bag of Doxorubicin, a very potent anti-cancer drug. It was really deceiving. It looked like orange Kool-Aid, but it was far from a thirst-quenching beverage.

The nurse was dressed in layers of protective gear: gloves, a mask and goggles. Maddie and I looked at each other, our eyes open as wide as saucers. Why all these safeguards? We were both too scared to ask the nurse why she needed to be so protected.

Seeing the looks of fear on our faces, the nurse tried to calm us, "Don't worry, we are specially trained to give the chemotherapy drug, the protective clothing is for handling the drug in case it leaks."

She hung the bag of Doxorubicin on Maddie's IV pole. It was to be administered over a forty-eight hour period directly into her veins.

The side effects could include hair loss, nausea, heart damage, bleeding, bruising, swelling, mouth sores and more. Another possible consequence was the risk of developing another type of cancer, such as leukemia, further down the road. Patients are only allowed to receive a limited amount of Doxorubicin during their lifetime because the cumulative effect can cause heart damage.

The doctors would carefully monitor Maddie. The side effects were alarming and scary. I needed to trust that this was the best course of action and that everyone knew what they were doing. I had to believe my daughter would be healed.

Maddie kept one eye on the drug, watching it drip. Then, seemingly bored, she turned her attention to the TV. After her show finished, Maddie decided to wander out to the hallway. The nurse came rushing over, "You can't leave your room," she said, blocking Maddie from going into the hallway. "Not till the chemo is finished transfusing," she said sternly.

She continued, "Once someone leaked some Doxorubicin from their IV tube and they had to evacuate the area, and later had to cut out the damaged carpet." As she said this, my eyes diverted over to the intravenous line. I watched this dangerous liquid, this poison, going directly into Maddie's veins.

Maddie looked at me with intense shock, panic spreading across her face. The nurse assured her she would be fine. As we sat back down, I couldn't help but wonder if what we were doing was right.

That night Maddie seemed okay, a little tired, but no nausea. We took this as a good sign. I moved my bed as close as I could to hers in case she woke up during the night. Thank goodness it was an uneventful evening.

The next morning she was able to eat her breakfast. She was a bit tired, and dozed off and on during the day. She was still not allowed to leave her room.

Her teacher from school, Blessed Kateri Tekakwitha, came to visit. Maddie's classmates had all made get well cards for her. Maddie was all smiles as she opened the large bag filled with the decorative cards.

"Get Well," "We Miss You," "Thinking of You," jumped out in brightly colored prints and sparkles. It was the last day of school, and they wanted Maddie to know they were thinking of her before they ventured off on their summer break.

Maddie smiled at her teacher, grateful for the good wishes, she said, "Miss, tell everyone 'thank you', and that I will be home soon, okay?" She taped the cards to the wall. There would be many days when all of these messages would become a voice of encouragement for her when she was really feeling lonely and down.

After her chemotherapy, we had to wait a few more days while they monitored Maddie to gauge her body's response to the drugs. On Sunday, we had a meeting with the doctor and nurse. We got great news: Maddie was stable enough to go home.

They gave us a lot of instructions— what to do, what to watch for, and what to expect during recuperation. The nurse cautioned us, "Expect to be in and out of the hospital on the days between treatments; it's not uncommon for that to happen."

"What type of problems?" I nervously asked.

"Well, Maddie may become too dehydrated and need fluids. She may need some pain control. She may become too sick to hold any food down. Don't worry. If these things happen, you just have to come to the emergency room. They will admit Maddie back to the floor for treatment. If she gets a fever, bring her back in right away," she explained.

I bought a monthly parking pass since we would be in and out so often. Parking was pretty expensive, money was tight, and this would be cheaper for us in the long run. We went down to the hospital parking garage. We got in the van and Maddie quickly turned the radio on to her favorite station. She leaned back and listened to the Nickelback's "Hero." I watched her relax as she enjoyed her music. I realized I needed to get her an iPod or something to help her pass the time while in the hospital.

7

Hair Today, Gone Tomorrow

We had been home about two days when I heard Maddie yell from her bedroom. "This is gross! Mom, come look."

Maddie was holding a hairbrush in her hand; she waved it in front of me. "Mom, it's happening, my hair is falling out!" We knew to expect this side-effect from the chemotherapy but it was heartbreaking to see the look of panic on her face. She had always taken pride in her beautiful, long brown hair. She had never cut it short. "Does this mean the chemo is working?" she asked.

"I think so," I answered, trying to sound positive.

"Okay. That's good then." she said, relieved. "What do we do now?"

"Try not to brush it too much. If it keeps coming out, we will figure something out."

"You mean shave my head?" she asked.

I didn't want to be the first one to speak about it, but since she had, I took advantage of the moment and said, "Yes dear, you might need to cut it off and get a wig." Then trying to soften the idea, I offered, "Maybe we can wait."

Her hair started showing up everywhere: long strands on the floor, chunks of it in the shower and on her clothes. "Mom, I'm shedding like a dog!" she exclaimed one day, sounding really annoyed.

"Do you want to make an appointment to get a wig?" I asked.

"I guess," she answered with very little enthusiasm. Who could blame her?

We had been told about a great program that generously supplied wigs at no cost to children with cancer. The wigs were made of donated, real human hair. I was so worried for Maddie. Would she feel embarrassed? What would this do to her self-esteem?

The day we went to look at wigs, we planned to make time to treat ourselves after she got it. We would go to the salon then out to lunch. The drive to Salon 244, in St. Catherine's, was uneventful. Maddie didn't say much. I was apprehensive; I prayed she wouldn't freak out. If she did, I knew I would lose it, too.

When we arrived, the staff greeted Maddie warmly and ushered her to the back room where the fitting would be done. Carlo, the owner, was a picture of kindness and chatted lightly with Maddie, very aware of the apprehension she was experiencing. He let her choose a wig, both the color and the length. Then, the moment was upon us. It was time to shave her head.

Maddie jumped right up in the chair. I held her hand and positioned myself in front of her. I wanted her to look at me and not the mirror; I thought I could shield her. Instead, she kept chattering away with Carlo about school, as if shaving her head was an everyday occurrence. Carlo first cut her hair short. It looked really cute, a style she had when she was really young. Then he picked up an electric trimmer and hesitated, waiting to make sure Maddie was ready. She joked with him, took a breath and then gave him a "thumbs-up" sign, and said, "Okay —go ahead."

He started at the top of her head, went down and across, past her ears. Each pass with the trimmer took more and more away, until what was left of her beautiful hair had vanished.

She looked radiant, and held her head high. I thought she was absolutely breathtaking. I looked at her stunning, shining blue eyes, her high cheek bones, and that smatter of freckles across her nose. She had naturally bright red lips, with a dimply smile that could melt the hardest of hearts. Tears filled my eyes as I looked at her. I couldn't make sense of it all. I kept thinking, "School's out. It's summer break. A twelve-year-old child should be at the beach or mall, not being fitted for a wig." I did not know what to say to comfort her.

As it turned out, I didn't have to say anything; she comforted me. Without any tears, she accepted this as something that had to be done. She smiled bravely through it all without an ounce of complaint.

"Do I need to wash it?" she asked Carlo about the wig.

"No, just brush it and store it on this," he told her, handing her a wig stand shaped like a head. "It will fit nice and snug and keep its shape."

"Maddie would you like me to shave my head, too?" I asked. I was ready to be as brave as she was. I would do anything to save her from feeling self-conscious. My hair was even longer than hers, almost to my waist. She loved my long hair.

"Mom, really!" she said. "Please . . . don't you dare. I'll be fine."

Carlo put the new wig on Maddie's head. It was the same color as her own hair and framed her face nicely. It was shoulder length, shorter than hers had been. It looked really natural. I couldn't tell the difference. She looked so cute.

"Let's take it for a trial run," I told her. "Let's get lunch." I was rushing her, wanting to get away from the sight of all her beautiful hair lying on the salon floor. We thanked Carlo and stepped out into the bright day. Maddie put on her sunglasses. She looked youthful and beautiful.

We went to a restaurant nearby and ordered a pizza. Maddie was nervously touching her head, making sure the wig wasn't moving around.

The waitress was really nice as she took our order. Maddie watched her vigilantly. Once she left, Maddie asked, anxiously, "Do you think she noticed?"

"Not at all," I replied.

"Good, I hope no one does."

Maddie was scheduled for her second round of chemo the next morning, which meant they would want us there at the hospital by early evening. I followed the hospital orders and called ahead of time to ensure Maddie had been booked with a room. The nurse apologized, saying they were not able to bring Maddie in for her scheduled chemo because there was a shortage of beds. They had forewarned us that on a rare occasion this might happen.

With this unexpected free night, Maddie and Derek were able to take advantage of an evening where she was feeling well enough to go for a swim in the back yard. We had a round, nine-foot, above-ground pool—nothing fancy. Maddie nervously took off her wig and tied a pink bandana on her head to hide her shaved head. She and Derek swam in the light of the moon, diving for glow sticks as they sunk to the bottom. They giggled and splashed around like it was any other normal summer evening. It was a wonderful sight. For a moment, life seemed simple and carefree. I wanted that moment to last forever.

As summer wore on, Maddie adjusted to life without her real hair, and eventually without the wig. She didn't trust that the wig would stay on when she was in the pool, and she didn't want it damaged. Plus it was itchy during extreme heat, so she seldom wore it. Her bald head drew stares from strangers. This bothered her initially but after a while she stopped noticing. Her medical challenges were instilling a resiliency and a maturity in her, way beyond her years.

8

Bravery Beads

For assessment between chemo treatments, Maddie was required to attend the outpatient clinic at McMaster Children's Hospital. We would go there once a week and the nurses on staff would monitor her blood count, give her IV fluids, and ensure she was stable. There were Child Life Specialists, trained to help normalize the hospital experience for the children in the Cancer Clinic.

They promoted a program called Bravery Beads for the oncology kids. The clinic provided colorful beads to the children so they could create their own beautiful and unique necklace representing their individual, special journey with cancer. The beads were symbolic, helpful tools to help each child tell his or her story. The children would build their necklaces as they progressed down their difficult road.

The first time Maddie went to the clinic, they gave her a cord on which to thread her bravery beads and showed her a bucket from which she could select the lettered beads that spelled her name.

Carefully digging through the container, she chose the six beads that spelled "MADDIE" and she showed them to me before she strung them on her necklace. Maddie loved crafts, and the idea of "earning" all these beads excited her. She sat next to the bucket and counted off all the treatments she had endured over the past few weeks, searching for the perfect bead to represent each experience. The long, brown ceramic one was for hair loss, the small, brown wooden ones for finger pokes, the small red ones for her chemotherapy, and the square blue one for getting her port-a-cath put in. She added each one to her cord. Her beautiful necklace was starting to take shape.

Over the year, she would collect different beads for each procedure or event she underwent while visiting the hospital. There were many different types of beads recognizing procedures and events such as hair loss, bone-marrow transplant, blood transfusions, radiation (this one glowed in the dark) and chemotherapy. Eventually she collected hundreds of beads.

Every time we were at the clinic, we noticed young children with their bravery beads, some hanging from their IV poles. Some children had rows and rows of beads. To an outsider unaware of the program and its meaning, the beads looked simply like pretty baubles, but we knew these beads told the story of the children's incredible bravery.

Maddie would always ask the other children about their beads. I saw how she really connected with each child and wanted to understand something about their personal story. She had such deep compassion for their pain and I realized that this was not a whimsical passing conversation, but rather her developing a deep awareness of human suffering.

In August, Maddie, Derek, Kevin, and I went to Camp Trillium for five days. This is a camp for children living with cancer, and their families. We arrived full of excitement as this was something that we felt would help balance our hospital life with perhaps a more normal experience.

Each family was assigned a special friend to help during their stay. Our friend was Becky, and it was her duty to assist us with programming each day and making sure that Maddie was feeling okay. There were so many activities for us to participate in: hiking, rock-climbing, ropes, kayaking, and swimming. You name it, this place provided it.

The purpose of the camp was to celebrate the healing process and bring families together. Everything was cause for celebration, and nothing was taken for granted—especially if it was towards the end of a child's chemotherapy treatment. In that case, the group would sing a special song and have a celebration cake. Since Maddie was just starting her chemo, the thought of her end-of-chemo celebrations seemed so very far down the road. But it was so nice to share in the success of the other children.

There was a large dining room where everyone would gather to share not only the daily feast but the antics of those with big personalities and big voices. Every evening was a highlight we looked forward to.

I had never seen another child with cancer before Maddie was diagnosed and it was overwhelming to see so many children, of all ages, in one place, struggling with the disease. Maddie was really sensitive to their plight, she always went out of her way to say "Hello," help with crafts, or hold a door open for someone. What bothered her the most was seeing really young children so sick.

Maddie often liked to challenge herself and one morning decided she was going to attempt climbing the high ropes and crossing a log that was positioned way up in the treetops. I was nervous, but let it go as I watched her. Becky and the staff ensured that Maddie was well secured in a climbing harness and gave her the go-ahead to climb. She easily got to the top and carefully made her way to the other side. I thought how perfect it was that she had reached a goal by herself, one that would give her confidence to know she could win when she put all her energy and heart into it.

On the last day we were there, Maddie and Becky went swimming together. Always looking out for Maddie's best interest, Becky asked her, "Are you wearing sunscreen?"

"Yes, of course," Maddie replied.

"Did you put some on your head too?" she asked, noting Maddie was not wearing her wig or a bandana.

"My head? Why?" Maddie responded feeling a bit confused.

"Because with no hair, you can sunburn your head, you have to be careful," Becky advised. "And, you need to make sure you put insect repellent on your arms and legs. too!"

"All right," Maddie said, swimming over to the edge of the pool to get the sunscreen. She paused, and with a quirky smile, looked back at Becky and said with a most serious tone, "If a mosquito bites me, would the mosquito get chemo?"

Becky shrugged her shoulders and said, "I don't know."

"Ha! Ha! Yes, it would have Mos-chemo!" Maddie said, laughing out loud. "Get it? Mosquito. Mos-chemo." They both laughed until they could hardly breathe.

The kids got lots of awards at camp. Maddie was a natural at catching frogs; she was so good that on our last night she was awarded a "#1 Frog-Catching Award" by the other campers.

There was also a talent show on the last night. Derek decided to enter and presented a Kung-Fu demonstration by breaking boards with his head. It was a pretty impressive accomplishment for an eight-year-old, and everyone cheered like crazy. (Unbeknownst to the audience, Uncle Kevin had sawed through the boards prior to the show.) The evening ended with a roaring bonfire. It was the perfect ending and the most memorable summer we would all share together.

When we returned home, Maddie's routine going back and forth to the hospital for chemo treatments and check-ups recommenced. School was soon to start, and Maddie was determined to attend the first day of eighth grade. She had difficulty keeping her food down after a round of chemotherapy, and the doctors decided it would be best for her to remain at the hospital. Stubbornly, she still insisted she be allowed to attend the first day of school.

"Mom, tell the doctors I'm fine," she pleaded. She couldn't wait to see all her friends. She was determined to be sitting in her classroom the first day. It became a test of wills between Maddie and the medical staff. They had warned us that if she was not keeping her food down, she could not be discharged, and they were sticking to their guns. She would eat and then unfortunately throw up a short time later. She then decided not to eat, that way, she wouldn't be sick and they couldn't stop her.

Tuesday morning, the first day of school, she pleaded with them again. The staff relented, and they let her go for the afternoon. Her teacher and classmates were ecstatic to see her back. She was there for one hour and returned back to the hospital to rest. We realized this is what the school year would probably be like while she was in treatment.

Maddie experienced good days and bad days. Balancing school and the "Evil Kool-Aid" treatments became her challenge.

She had started her treatments in June, and it was now September. This meant we had three months down and nine to go. Her bravery-bead necklace was getting longer and heavier.

9

Puppy Love

After three months of chemo to reduce the size of the tumor, the doctors were pleased enough with the results that they decided it was time to attempt to remove it. The surgery was scheduled for 8.00 A.M. on October 1st. I met with the surgeon to discuss the procedure. They still weren't sure how invasive the tumor was or how aggressive the surgery would need to be until they opened her up.

We told Maddie the procedure would take a few hours and that the surgeon would do his best to remove the whole tumor. I didn't feel it was in her best interest to worry her with all the potentially difficult scenarios because no one really knew what they would find or need to do.

The night before the surgery, we threw caution to the wind. We visited friends and kept Maddie up late driving ATV's in the countryside. It was a new experience for her. She proved to be a good driver, but with the recent rain, she got stuck in the mud and had to be pushed out. She loved it. We sat in an open field and watched the sun set, everyone laughing and talking, just enjoying our time together.

My hope was that we would exhaust her so she would be too tired to worry about the impending surgery. I don't know if it really worked, but each time I checked on her during the night, Maddie was fast asleep.

We were up early the morning of the surgery. The drive to the hospital was unusually quiet—both of us were lost in our thoughts. We had learned to become comfortable with the silence, not needing to say anything just for the sake of saying something.

When arrived at the hospital, the staff greeted us and started to take Maddie away to prep her for the surgery.

"Maddie, do you want me to come in the operating room with you, until they put you under?" I asked, wanting to help in some way.

"Yes, Mom, hold my hand and don't let go, okay?" she asked. Turning to the nurse, she insisted, "You have to let my mom come, too."

"Absolutely," the nurse replied.

I was relieved they'd let me in the operating room with her until she was sedated. Dressed in my hospital scrubs, I entered a room full of machines and equipment, all humming and making loud noises, all waiting for my dear Maddie. I don't know why, but I was shocked by the sight. I could only imagine how frightened Maddie must be.

The team of medical professionals were standing by preparing for the surgery. Overwhelmed, I quietly prayed that they would take good care of my little girl. She was lying on the table, nurses were on both sides of her explaining what was coming next.

One said, "We will start the anesthesia now, you won't feel anything, just let yourself go to sleep."

I gently held her hand. "How are you feeling Maddie? I asked.

"I'm okay," she answered, softly, with a slight smile for me.

"I'm right here, I'm going to hold your hand and not let go until you go to sleep. When you awake, I will be here."

"Okay, Mom."

"Maddie, count backwards from 100 for me," instructed the nurse.

"One hundred, ninety nine, ninety eight…"

"I love you!" I whispered in her ear as I leaned in and kissed her forehead.

A nurse chaperoned me out of the operating theatre and ushered me to the changing room. I was numb—on autopilot. I removed the hospital scrubs, composed myself as best I could, and went to the waiting room where my family had already gathered. I collapsed in my mother's arms; the same arms that had comforted me when my husband died.

We knew the surgery was going to be quite involved and could potentially take all day. The surgeons felt it might be necessary to remove up to three ribs and part of her left lung in order to remove as much of the tumor as possible. The tumor was pushing up against Maddie's spine and lung which meant that the surgeons had to be especially cautious during the removal. The consequences could include paralysis.

We were prepared that she would be in the ICU (Intensive Care Unit) for some time, after which she would be transferred to the step-down ward 3C. The surgery took from 8:00 A.M. until 7:00 P.M., but we received updates throughout the day. Around dinnertime, we were told that the tumor had been successfully removed, intact. The tumor had been attached to her left lung, so they did have to remove part of her lung; they also did remove three ribs. They had to cut through a few nerves that were encased in the tumor and we were told she would experience some loss of feeling in her chest area. There was nerve damage to her left arm along with one nerve they had to scrape; they did not want to compromise the use of her arm and they did the best they could.

We were told there was a possibility that a few cancer cells had been left in Maddie's body, and they would send samples to pathology to see if she would need to undergo radiation.

As they wheeled Maddie out of the operating room to transfer her to the ICU, I jumped up and stopped them so that I could see her. I didn't recognize her at first; she had a little knitted hat on to keep her head warm where her hair used to be. Machines were hooked up everywhere and attached to the bed. I couldn't get close to her. I wanted to hold her—to let her know everything would be all right.

They asked me to wait outside while they settled Maddie into the ICU. I waited fifteen minutes and then I entered the room. Maddie was restrained and tied to the bed. There were machines and tubes surrounding her. She was on a ventilator. I stared in disbelief as I realized she was awake, tears running down her face. Her eyes seemed to be begging me to remove the breathing tube. I knew she felt she was choking.

They had told me that she would still be sedated. I couldn't believe that she was awake. She should have been asleep. After I complained and begged them to knock her out again, they finally gave her sedatives that sent her into a deep sleep.

Over the next four days, while recovering in ICU, she had an ongoing problem with pain. She had seventy staples in her back. To help her control the pain, she was given a morphine pump that she controlled herself. Her body was swollen. As her swelling came down, she was slowly weaned off the ventilator. During this time, her only means of communication was her smile and barely a whisper that said thank you to everyone around her as they assisted with her care.

Eventually the morphine they gave her caused Maddie to have delusions. She hallucinated when she was awake, and she would wake up screaming when she tried to sleep. Someone had given her a stuffed orangutan, which occupied a tiny place at the end of her bed.

One evening as she was waking up, she looked down at him and had a total meltdown. After that, we hid all the stuffed animals from her.

She stayed in the ICU for about a week. There are no couches or pull-outs in the unit; we had to sleep in chairs, by her bed. Kevin never left her side; Susan would come in between shifts at work, usually without any sleep. We would take turns stretching out on the couches in the waiting room. Sometimes, we would wander the halls, opening doors looking for an empty room with a cot or a chair to curl up in it. None of us wanted to leave Maddie, not even for a moment.

She would come around for a few minutes and I wanted to make sure that someone was with her. The nurses woke her hourly to check how she was feeling. By the fourth day she could sit up with some help. She wasn't eating but she did manage to take sips of water. Her pain was always an issue, difficult to manage.

She was finally moved to the step-down ward from the ICU, where there were more nurses per patient than in the regular wards. Maddie and the machines that were attached to her still needed to be monitored closely.

There was a constant back and forth of doctors, surgeons, and pain-control teams in and out of the room. Maddie complained that she could not get comfortable. The doctor had told me that getting your ribs removed is one of the most painful procedures. It devastated me that Maddie had to find that out at such a young age. She had tubes everywhere: catheters, IVs, and drainage tubes for her lungs. Her left lung, the one they removed a portion of, had collapsed. She was still on oxygen. The staples in her back made her itch. I was her official backscratcher.

After a week, she started to come around. Her spirits were up; she began joking with the staff, and thanking them for all they were doing. She needed less and less morphine, her appetite was back. They finally removed her catheter, and she was free to walk to the bathroom. She watched TV, read a bit, and even asked about her homework.

When the staples were ready to be removed, Maddie smiled as she read the nameplate of the nurse who entered the room. It read "D. R. Staples."

"Hey, Dr. Staples," Maddie laughed.

"No Maddie, I'm not a doctor, I'm a nurse. My initials are D. R."

"Okay, Dr. Staples, if you say so," Maddie giggled.

The doctors were undecided if Maddie needed to undergo radiation. Although they had removed the tumor completely, they still need to ensure that there was a specific radius of cancer-free skin around the tumor—what they called "a clear margin." They consulted with the doctors who were controlling the study in the US to have them decide if she needed the radiation.

We were cautioned that if she was to start radiation, it was to be done no later than two weeks after the surgery. This was due to their concern that there might be a few cancer cells that had been disturbed and were floating around in her body. Since time was of the essence, they started preparing for this contingency.

When Maddie came home after eleven days in the hospital, there was a very special gift waiting for her; it was a new puppy.

The puppy had been delivered to our home a week earlier, while Maddie was still in the hospital. When Maddie and I walked into the house, Derek handed the tiny ball of fur to Maddie. She laughed when she saw it, and held him gently. He was a pug, fawn colored, with black markings on his face. He started to lick Maddie's face, happy to meet her. Maddie bonded with the little guy right away. He was adorable, and so tiny; he fit right in the palm of her hand. Because of his appearance, he was rightfully named after Winston Churchill.

She spent her time sitting on the floor, trying to train him and get him to obey. "Winston, come. Winston, sit," Maddie demanded. Her commands fell on deaf ears, but she didn't care. She would play with him for hours. Her pain seemed to lessen when she was with him. Her focus was more on her dog than her illness. He would nuzzle under her chin and sleep there. She wouldn't dare move, in case she woke him. He was still too small to take for a walk outside, so Maddie opted to walk him up and down the hallway.

Maddie was only home for two days when she began to experience nerve pain that could not be controlled with the oral medications; she needed the morphine pump again.

"Mom, when I go back to the hospital, can you sneak Winston in for a visit?" she pleaded, not wanting to be away from him.

"Sorry Maddie, we can't risk it, there are really sick kids there and some may be allergic," I said.

"Okay, I understand," she agreed, yet she was disappointed.

She loved her new puppy and so she posed with Winston for a picture. She would carry it with her; it would be a comfort to her while they were apart.

10

Dear Oprah

When the pathology report came back, it indicated that the surgeons hadn't achieved the safety margin during the surgery. They had been very, very close, but hadn't been able to cut any closer to the spine for risk of paralysis. Maddie needed to start radiation right away. The news was a horrible disappointment. Maddie had barely begun to recover from the surgery and now she would have to walk through a new set of hospital doors.

The radiation would be administered in the mornings followed by a toxic cocktail of chemotherapy in the afternoons. I was frightfully worried at the toll this was taking on Maddie's already frail body. The doctors were insistent that her disease needed to be treated aggressively.

Maddie was now a patient at the JCC the Juravinski Cancer Centre on Hamilton Mountain. Fortunately, the center was only ten minutes from our home. The protocol was to administer five weeks of daily radiation, in addition to the chemotherapy. I was sickened by the thought of Maddie suffering through this. She was only thirteen years old, how could she possibly handle it all? Whenever I brought up the subject of her treatments she would quietly dismiss me. She never wanted to discuss them. She stoically did what she had to do.

The doctors wanted to have a foam body cast made that would keep Maddie completely still while the radiation was targeted on the area around her spine. The technician instructed her to raise her arm over her head.

"I can't," Maddie said apologetically. "I really can't, it hurts too much."

"Try again. We really need to make this mold in order for your treatment to be successful."

"I'm really trying," Maddie said with tears in her eyes. "I just can't raise my arm."

"Well if you can't do it, we won't be able to make the body mold." His words were firm but kind, as he truly wanted to convince Maddie that this had to be done.

In a timid and defeated voice she again said, "I'm sorry. I can't raise my arm no matter how many times you ask me." She looked at me with pleading eyes to help her make him understand.

"She can't do it, so what's the alternative?" I calmly interjected.

"Well, we can to do it without the mold, but we would rather not." With his eyes fixated on Maddie he said firmly, "You will have to be *really* still."

"Okay," she replied, relieved this matter was now resolved and not open for further discussion.

Not knowing anything about the process, I was worried that we might compromise the effectiveness of her treatment; they assured me this was not the case.

On the morning of her first treatment Maddie had an odd little grin on her face; it was like she had a secret—one I wasn't in on. As we drove to the center, I noticed that the little grin was still there and so I asked, "Maddie, what's up? Are you hiding something from me?"

Laughing, she said, "Mom, I am getting a tattoo today."

She had often threatened that one day she was going to get a tattoo and a lip ring. I had repeatedly assured her that was *never* going to be an option.

Puzzled, I looked at her and said, "Really? *Mmmhmmm*."

"Yup. I am and there is nothing you can say or do about it." She said grinning.

We got to the center and they wheeled Maddie into the treatment room. The doctor said, "Mrs. Babineau, we will now begin prepping Maddie for her tattoo." I nearly fainted.

"Really?" I said, bewildered.

The doctor proceeded to explain that they would need to mark the exact area where the laser beam emitting the radiation would line up. The only way to ensure the accuracy of the laser would to create three very small tattoos on Maddie's back. The doctors confirmed that a lip ring was not part of the deal.

Soon after Maddie began her radiation treatments, we started trips between the Juravinski Cancer Centre and McMaster Children's Hospital for her follow-up chemo treatments. Depending on the day's schedule, Maddie would often be transported by ambulance between the two centers. It only took a few trips before Maddie had her own fan club among the paramedics. They jokingly fought over who would take her back and forth. Somehow, she managed to hide her pain and suffering with her infectious smile, and her witty charm captivated all of them.

Maddie loved clothes and had several T-shirts with off-the-wall sayings on them. Her favorite was, "Boys are smelly and come from the smelly factory." She always got a rise out of the male paramedics when she wore it, innocently asking them, "Do you like my shirt?" And, of course, they humored her with their encouraging laughter. Another favorite T-shirt was a picture of a goth girl holding an empty ice cream cone, the ice cream melted on the sidewalk below her feet. The caption read, "This is the poopiest of days." Maddie wore this one on the days of her chemotherapy treatment.

When the paramedics wheeled her through the hospital corridors, passing by the cafeteria with the colorful displays of all treats imaginable, she would say, "Oh! Don't those Rice Krispie treats look amazing?" On the next run, Maddie would find a little bag of treats in the back of the ambulance beside her stretcher. There was no question she had figured out how to win their hearts with her gentle persuasion.

One day, during a routine ambulance run, the driver cleverly gifted Maddie with one of her happiest moments. Under his uniform, he wore a T-shirt he had made that said, "Girls are smelly too." When she saw it, Maddie laughed so hard that I thought she would fall off the stretcher. I smiled and was grateful to know how many kind and thoughtful people were in our lives.

One day when my daughter was sleeping, I was watching *The Oprah Winfrey Show* on TV. Oprah talked about a new program called "Dreams Come True." She was taking a bus on the road to meet people and fulfill their wishes. I felt like the segment was a call to action. It seemed like the perfect idea to take Maddie somewhere that would bring some joy into her life, and make her forget her trials—if at least for a few hours.

I wrote to the show, detailing Maddie's journey with cancer as well as her relationship with her dad and his ALS, and seeking Oprah's assistance in getting Maddie to go see the MTV awards show. I wasn't convinced I would even get an answer, but I had to believe it was possible. I had nothing to lose.

I wanted to make sure the package I sent would stand out and grab someone's attention. I wrapped it in fluorescent pink wrapping paper, included Maddie's picture on the outside and a note about her story. I said a prayer, and sent the package off in the mail, hoping it would get there safely.

A few months later, Maddie and I sat together watching Oprah's season opening show—the one where she surprised people with the opportunity to make their dreams come true. I realized then that my wish had not been fulfilled. The lucky winners had already been informed. I watched the show, thinking how so many people's lives were being changed.

While the show was on, our daily mail arrived and I retrieved it during a commercial break. I was surprised to see a parcel included amongst the letters. The parcel was addressed: "To the Young Girl with Cancer." How unusual and odd I thought.

I brought the parcel to Maddie.

"What is it?" she asked.

As I handed it to her, I shared how I had written to the Oprah Show and how I had hoped that Maddie would have been one of the people on the season opener.

Maddie looked stunned, jumped up and squealed, "Mom, you are so embarrassing! Did you *really* write to Oprah? I can't believe it!"

Although astonished by my boldness, I knew she would have loved the opportunity. "Yes, I did. I wanted to surprise you. But I have no idea who sent this package, hurry, open it!"

"Oh my goodness, what could it be?" she asked. Maddie placed the box on her lap and very methodically unwrapped it. A card inside read: "We were touched by your parcel. We are thinking of you. We hope your dreams do come true."

Enclosed was a gift card to a retail store with a handwritten message, "Please buy yourself a new outfit to wear on the Oprah Show!" Inside the box was a beautiful statue of the Angel of Hope. The card was signed by the postal workers at the Kitchener, Ontario, postage depot.

Maddie held the wooden angel, "Mom, this is really nice. I can't believe they did this," Maddie said truly humbled.

"How did they find me?" she asked, puzzled.

I began to think through the process and realized that somehow my parcel to Oprah must have been cleared through the Kitchener station. Wow, Maddie and I both shook our heads. She said, "We need to thank them and meet them!"

"Maybe we can track them down!" Maddie said as she placed the wooden angel on the mantle in the living room.

The following day, I called the local Hamilton TV station CHCH TV. I shared the goodwill story and how I thought a news clip about the package would be a wonderful way to acknowledge the postal workers' generosity. The producer agreed. They arranged the meeting and captured it on video for the evening news. Maddie and I drove to the processing centre and met the most amazing group of people led by one wonderful woman who was touched by Maddie's story.

She explained what had happened. Out of the corner of her eye she had caught a glimpse of something that was clearly not where it should have been. It was a box that had been wedged out of sight in between a table and the sorting room wall. The bright pink paper caught her attention. She reached down and pulled it out. She read the outside of the package and realized this was actually addressed to Oprah Winfrey. As she read further she realized that this was no ordinary piece of mail. This was a magical request by a mother for her daughter who was living with cancer.

She told us that what hit her in that moment was how she had been feeling sorry for herself. Seeing the package had helped put her own problems in perspective. Maddie's world became a source of inspiration for her to see her own life with new eyes.

Maddie blushed as she listened to the woman, and once more felt the love and support of strangers. "Thank you," she said as we prepared to leave. "I will always cherish the beautiful angel you sent me." She hugged them and left the building, wearing a great big smile.

11

Hope for the Holidays

*T*he trips to the hospital were becoming more and more difficult. Not only was Maddie suffering from the lingering pains from her surgery, but the ill effects of her chemo and radiation were taking their toll. She was extremely weak and nauseous. Getting in and out of the car in the harsh winter weather added to her discomfort. To top it off, the layers of bulky winter clothing made it difficult for her frail body to move.

She now barely weighed ninety-five pounds. She wasn't eating; the skin on her back was burned from the radiation and was raw and sore. Nevertheless, she never really complained. She would apologize for sleeping all the time and not being good company. Maddie was convinced we were suffering because of her. Eventually, she was not longer able to take Winston out for walks or to feed him. She just didn't have the strength.

Her radiation sessions finally ended just before Christmas 2004, and she also got a break from her chemo treatments. Christmas was one of her favorite times of the year. She loved baking and creating little gift bags for every place setting at the dinner table. Although this particular Christmas was expected to be rather low key, it held the most importance as we were all together as a family.

"Mom, will you take Derek and me to the mall, please?" she asked. "We need to buy gifts and he's going to help me. Oh, yes… and could you loan me some money? I'm pretty sure I have some allowance coming to me."

I was happy to see her enthusiasm, especially her wanting to spend time with her brother. Derek helped me get her into the car; we placed her wheelchair in the trunk and off we went.

I dropped them off at the mall entrance and went to park the car. When I returned, I saw Derek and Maddie busily chatting at one of the kiosks. The walls were filled with fragile and dainty blown-glass figurines. Maddie saw me first, and held up her hand, "Mom, don't come any closer," she warned. "Derek is picking out your gift!"

I stepped back and watched from afar, holding my breath as Derek moved around the overstocked table. I watched his puffy winter coat nearly graze the row of fragile figurines. The sales clerk approached him, and he pointed out the figurine he wanted. She wrapped it up and he paid for it. I couldn't see what is was, but the gift was already given. Just watching them together meant more than any gift I could ever receive.

Derek had turned nine the week before; we found a great little restaurant and celebrated his birthday over lunch. Maddie barely ate, but all of us being together was what was important to her. We finished our shopping and we headed home to begin our festivities.

Although Maddie's energy was low, she still wanted to help me prepare Christmas dinner, decorate, and to wrap presents. She came out of her bedroom holding an odd-shaped gift and placed it under the tree. I couldn't recognize it from what she had purchased earlier.

"What is that Maddie?" I asked.

"It's a bone for Winston, I want to surprise him and don't want the shape to give it away, so I wrapped it over and over again!" she said laughing.

It was wonderful that Maddie could be home for Christmas, and not at the hospital. We spent the day with family and friends exchanging gifts. Her school friends visited and she got the scoop on what everyone had been up to. All of this was music to her ears. She inhaled every word they shared, all the stories and gossip about school. There is little doubt in my mind that she missed being part of that world, but you would never know it as she smiled and laughed and embraced it all.

Our joy was short lived. Maddie became very ill the next day. We went back to the hospital and she was admitted through the emergency room. She was kept in isolation, and had a high fever Her immune system was wiped out. I thought, "Can it get any worse?"

Within twenty-four hours she contracted the Norwalk virus.

Later in the week, I reluctantly left her to run an errand. Susan offered to stay with Maddie; she loved to spend time with her. I was gone about an hour and when I returned Susan was sitting in the hallway, outside Maddie's door.

"What's up?" I asked, a bit surprised to see her there.

"Oh, I'm in time-out," she answered, looking all serious.

"What happened?"

"Well, you know the show, *Dancing with the Stars*?"

"Yes, we've watched it."

"Well, I was watching it with Maddie and I kept making fun of the dancers . . ."

"Aren't we supposed to?" I interrupted, in agreement.

"Apparently not, Maddie said I was being very mean and to stop it right away, then she kicked me out of her room!"

"Did she really?" I asked astonished by such boldness.

"No. Not really, almost though," Susan laughed. "Her nurse is fixing her bed, so I came out for a minute. Just be warned, if you're going to watch the show with her, be nice," she advised.

I laughed as I thought how I, too, was guilty. Maddie is so pure in heart she must be the only one on the planet who doesn't make fun of the dancers on the show. As I stepped in to the room to greet her, I made sure I was on my best behavior.

We celebrated New Year's Eve in the hospital. Uncle Kevin, always working hard to keep Maddie in good spirits, showed up with a party package of hats, confetti and noise-makers. We ignored our surroundings and created a celebration that Maddie, Derek, Uncle Kevin and I would never be able to repeat or forget.

Maddie couldn't eat because of painful ulcers in her mouth, but it didn't stop her from beckoning in the New Year with a courageous smile.

"Wait!" Maddie cried out just before we started to celebrate. "You can't blow noise-makers here, we will wake everyone up!"

"Good point," said Uncle Kevin. "I can fix that." He carefully removed the sound pieces thus disabling the noise. As midnight approached, we looked ridiculous: blowing as hard as we could on the noise makers, not making a peep, and turning blue in the process. We had our hats on, and we threw confetti around the whole room. Deep in my heart I held onto this moment as a celebration of how precious our time together was. It was a good way to start the New Year.

12

The Wish

*T*he winter months went by and the cycle continued: chemotherapy treatments, sickness, coming home to recover, returning to the hospital when she was too sick.

Most days, all Maddie could muster was enough energy to turn on the TV. I would think to myself, *What is going through her mind? What could begin to even interest her at this stage?*

One quiet afternoon, as she was repeatedly flipped through the channels, she saw an image that forced her to freeze. It was a show about the difficult plight of the children in Africa. She sat up in her hospital bed and watched in raptured silence. On screen, a young boy was walking down a long dusty road. He appeared hungry, afraid and alone. A harsh reality about life halfway around the world was being played out in front of Maddie's eyes.

She was stunned by what she witnessed. Here she was battling her own life-threatening disease and yet something inside of her set that aside. The show brought to light the daily hardships that children in a particular village in East Africa were coping with: stories about how they walked for miles between villages to collect water. Many were homeless, not able to attend school, as they had to work to survive. The faces of starving children going to bed hungry made an impression on Maddie that ripped through her being. She watched with horror as the images of frail, orphaned, and struggling children panned over and over.

Maddie was especially moved by a lonely young boy.

"Mom, this is so sad. Look he's only six years old and he has nobody to care for him. I cannot imagine being so alone." She looked up at me, her sad eyes wide open. For a split second, I recognized fear in those pristine blues, but it quickly abated when she fell into my arms as I lay quietly beside her. Maddie knew she was more than safe and not alone. With a sigh of relief she gazed up at me and whispered, "Mommy, I am so grateful I have you. I couldn't imagine life without at least one parent." I closed my eyes and thanked the universe for giving me this angel.

Maddie knew what it was like to go hungry, not because we lacked food, but because the side-effects of the chemotherapy left her extremely nauseated and unable to eat.

Today, I believe that Maddie felt more than empathy for that young boy. She connected with him in a deep and mysterious way that ultimately changed all of our lives. As the show became increasingly difficult for me to watch, I noticed that Maddie was mesmerized and made no attempt to change the channel. She watched until the very end. She saw the ugliness of poverty, the flies, the bloated bellies, and the desperate faces open to the camera, silently pleading for help.

Though sick herself, she heard their silent pleas from across the ocean. She clearly understood their suffering and knew they needed help—her help.

"Mom, how can this happen? What will happen to this boy? Do you think he is still alive?" She had so many questions. Watching the show had made her anxious, and her mind was racing.

Maddie knew she had to do something. She didn't know how it would happen, but she made a promise to help those children and make a difference in their lives.

We were interrupted by the nurse coming in to prepare Maddie for more chemo. As she wheeled her out of the room I offered a gentle nudge. "Maddie, one day at a time sweetheart, let's get you better first."

She smiled and said, "Yes Mommy, when I'm feeling better."

Two weeks later, back in the hospital for more treatment, Maddie was inspired by another TV documentary—this one about a young man named Craig Kielburger. When Craig was twelve years old, he had started Free the Children, an organization of "children helping children through education."

He had been inspired to act when he read about a boy named Iqbal, a young Pakistani who was sold in a *peshgi* bet (loan) for twelve dollars. He lived a life of slavery, making rugs, until he escaped at the age of ten. He started speaking out about the issue of child labor and as a result was shot dead in the streets of his hometown, at the age of twelve.

Craig had been so horrified by this story that it moved him to take action. He took the newspaper article into his classroom and asked his classmates if they would join him in trying to do something about child labor. At the end of the class, eleven hands went up, twelve including his. This small group of twelve, twelve-year-olds was the beginning of what is now one of the most important organizations in the world.

Maddie was fascinated by what Craig had accomplished. She noted that Craig was twelve when he was moved to take action. Iqbal was twelve when he spoke out against child labor, and she, too, was twelve when she was diagnosed with cancer. Their stories inspired her to believe in the power of twelve-year-olds. Craig lived only an hour away and Maddie hoped that maybe one day they would meet.

Later that month, back for another session of chemotherapy, there was a knock on Maddie's hospital room door. She rarely received visitors at this time of the day. It was Julia, one of the Child Life Specialists. She said, "Maddie I have great news for you." Maddie quickly sat up, very interested in what she had to say.

"If you could have a wish, what would it be?" Julia asked.

"I don't know." Maddie replied puzzled.

"Well just think for a moment. If you were granted a wish, what would you wish for?"

"How can I have a wish?" Maddie asked, "Do you have special powers like Aladdin's magic lamp?" she laughed

"No," Julia said smiling, looking Maddie squarely in the face. "Have you heard of the Children's Wish Foundation?"

"No." Maddie was now excited and curious.

Julia sat at the side of Maddie's bed and began to explain to her. "They are an organization that provides children who are very sick the opportunity to realize their most heartfelt wish."

"Like what?" Maddie asked with genuine interest.

"Well, some children have asked for a Disney Cruise or a laptop for school, or even a $5,000 shopping spree!" she said, and continued, "They've contacted us to let you know that you're now on their list. You can have any wish you want." Julia beamed as she gave Maddie the news.

"Wow, this is amazing," Maddie said. It truly seemed like Aladdin's magic lamp. Maddie could have anything she wanted.

"Do I have to pick it right now?" she asked, worried she would have to make such a big decision on the spot.

"No, take your time; let me know when you are ready." And on that note, she gave Maddie a hug and left the room.

Maddie turned to me with an ear-to-ear smile. "Mom, can you believe it? I get to have a wish!"

To be granted a wish was a dream come true for her. She danced, gingerly, around the room, saying, "I get a wish! I get a wish!"

Her young and imaginative mind quickly started to list the endless possibilities. It could be the answer to all the things that she had longed for in the past. All the things we could never afford.

She took a few days to contemplate and dream of all the possibilities this magical wish could bring her. She could have a new wardrobe, meet a movie star, or take a great vacation; anything she wanted.

"Mom, I could go to the amazing Atlantis Resort." She had seen pictures of it once in a magazine, "Or, I could meet Wade." Maddie dreamt of one day meeting her favorite hockey player in the world, Wade Redden of the Ottawa Senators.

I enjoyed watching her as her thoughts danced from one idea to another and delighted in seeing her smile once again.

She couldn't wait to finish her treatment so she could go home and tell her brother.

Once home, she burst through the door and squealed, "Derek, you won't believe this. I got a wish, an actual wish!" She breathlessly shared the good news with him. "Anything that I want . . . isn't that amazing?

"Don't worry, if I take the $5,000 shopping spree, I will make sure I get you something really cool," she said, always wanting to share her good fortune. "Just don't let Mom pick out your clothes," she whispered to him.

The next few days were full of the buzz and excitement of Maddie's wish. She looked for ideas online and in magazines. Everyone who found out had myriad ideas and suggestions. Even Winston seemed aware that something special was happening. I think if he had understood, he would have requested an unending supply of bones.

As Maddie thought through all the wonderful possibilities, her mind kept going back to what she had witnessed on TV: the suffering children in Africa. She kept returning to how terribly wrong it was and how it made her feel so sad at how helpless they were. She once again wondered if she could do something for them.

A few days later, she came into my room, sat beside me on my bed and said, "Mommy, there are a ton of things I would like to have, but honestly, I don't need anything!"

Without taking a breath and with a sparkle in her eye she exclaimed, "I really would like to make this wish very special." She paused.

"I want to give my wish away! I want to give it to the little boy I saw on TV... and all the other children who have nothing! I want to use it to make their lives a little better," she said, adding, "I want my wish to be meaningful; to make a difference in the lives of the children in Africa. When I give them my wish, I give them hope. My wish could fulfill their wish. This makes it a perfect wish. Do you think it will be okay? To give it away?" she asked, quickly taking in a breath of air. Her eyes shone as she continued, "I want to share this once-in-a-lifetime special wish."

"Maddie that sounds wonderful." I was surprised and delighted by her sincere gesture.

"How can I use my wish to help them?" she wondered. "I'm too sick to go to Africa, what else can I do?" As she thought back to the program we had watched, Maddie remembered that schools were the key to breaking the cycle of poverty. She decided what she wanted to do, but she would need help.

"Mom, Maybe I can ask Craig Kielburger and his organization to help me. We have to call him. Can you find their number for me please," she asked, all excited.

I searched and found the number online, dialed the phone, and passed it to her.

"Hello," said a voice on the other line.

"Do you build schools?" she shyly asked.

The person on the other end simply said, "Yes."

"In Africa?"

"Yes, in Kenya," the young woman answered.

"Perfect." Maddie was so excited she hung up without saying good-bye, her mind filled with hope for the potential her wish could bring.

"Mom, I'm going to build a school in Africa with my wish!" she announced, so delighted by the idea. She jumped up and ran down the hall to share her vision with Derek.

Maddie now had a plan. She knew exactly what she would do. She would use her wish to build a school in Africa and help the children by giving them an education.

I, too, believed she could do it. But first, we had to get her better. That was *my* wish.

13

Hope Lives

Maddie's energy intensified. It was clear to all of us that her excitement about the project in Africa was making the difference. She became a much happier person with the incentive that she was going to help the children in the third world. It helped her take the focus off of the cancer and let her channel her energies into something wonderful and positive. Her wish was actually giving back to her, filling her big heart with purpose.

We had no idea at the time how this miracle wish would grow, nor did we understand there was so much magic in Maddie's wisdom.

Free the Children had already successfully built numerous schools in Africa so they agreed to partner with Maddie to make her wish a reality. She was invited and encouraged to discuss the planning and location of the school with the staff. She learned where in Africa her school would be built, and she was able to choose which grade the one room classroom would teach: It would be built for seventh-grade students.

Finally, the Children's Wish Foundation sent Maddie an official letter: her wish to build the school had been approved. Now, her own personal goal was in motion.

As I observed her, I was torn between pain and joy. It was very difficult to see my beautiful daughter suffer her physical torment, as the cancer took control of much of her life. But it was heartwarming to watch her as the gift of her wish enabled Maddie to focus her energy on building something that was real and meaningful to her.

Maddie had always been a very kind child, but this level of caring seemed extraordinary. She was becoming a global humanitarian as she exercised her understanding about the injustices dealt the children in Africa.

Maddie was fired up and she looked to Craig as her role model. She began to find confidence in her own voice and convictions. She started to overcome her shyness by calling him to arrange a visit so she could meet him personally.

Maddie and Craig quickly became friends, first by phone and then email. She worked expediently and quietly with him on the school project. She was not about fanfare or media attention. She asked that we honor her request that no one was to know she was doing this.

Maddie continued her treatment throughout that spring. On May 10, 2005, we finally celebrated; it was Maddie's last chemotherapy session. She had endured this lifestyle long enough. When we arrived at the hospital there was a big banner on Maddie's door proclaiming "Congratulations Maddie" courtesy of the wonderful staff.

"I'm glad this is over," she excitedly said. "I can't wait to be normal again, no more hospitals."

She took her banner and began skipping instead of walking down the hallways, stopping to get everyone who had helped her over the past year sign it. She thanked each of them, one by one, for their help. When she had thanked each person, she returned to her room and began packing up her hospital life: her crafts, the gifts she had received, and the hundreds of get-well cards. She carefully removed her bravery beads from her I.V. pole. They had multiplied into many strands with hundreds of colorful beads. She placed them around her neck; a year's worth. The beads silently said it all: Maddie was a survivor who had bravely endured a very long battle.

Almost one month after settling into a "normal life," Maddie heard about the Relay for Life event. It was an all-night team fundraiser for the Canadian Cancer Society, and it was happening in our community. She wanted to celebrate, to do something positive. It was June 17, 2005: the one-year anniversary of the day that we found out about Maddie's tumor.

Giving away her wish had left her with a greater sense of accomplishment, and renewed confidence to reach out and do something else meaningful.

"Mom, I want to give back. Remember the walk-a-thon we used to do for dad every summer? Can we do this one for cancer research, now?" she pleaded, showing me the flyer.

"Maddie, it's an all-night walk, how can you possibly physically accomplish this?"

"What if I ask all my friends? We can be a team," she said with a look of something beyond determination. I knew I had no say in this and would never be able to change her mind.

The next day, she went to school and asked her classmates if they would join her in an all-night relay for cancer.

Although she hated to speak in front people, she went to the front of the class, and with a tremble in her voice asked: "Please, join me and walk for cancer research." Her bald head and compassionate look said it all; this was important to her. One by one the children's hands went up. The whole class agreed to walk with Maddie. She was ecstatic.

All her classmates joined her on that magical night, a night when Maddie got to fight back and raise funds for a cure for cancer. This was a great way to celebrate her end of treatment.

The Relay for Life was twelve hours, (7:00 P.M. to 7:00 A.M.). It was held at the Dofasco Recreation Center and the participants would walk around the outdoor track. Still weak from her final round of chemo, Maddie used her wheelchair to get around. Her team, Maddie and Friends, pushed her. My team was made up of girlfriends from my baseball team and we were known as Moms for Maddie. We stayed up, talking, walking, and listening to bands all night.

At the beginning of the event there was a special and very touching survivor walk. Each survivor was to carry a baton around the first lap, then pass it on to their teams. Maddie was waiting at the starting line. I was going to push her around in her wheelchair when suddenly she put her foot out and stopped me.

She turned around, straining her neck as she looked out into the crowd for her Nanny and Uncle Kevin. When she saw them, she called out, "Nanny and Uncle Kevin, come quick and join me!" They were her heroes. They had survived cancer and they had given her hope during her treatment. She wanted to walk side by side with them.

I stepped aside and proudly watched as my mother and brother accompanied Maddie on the survivor lap. You could not help but be humbled watching the strength and courage of all the survivors as they walked proudly and circled the track.

The kids were going strong, enjoying the warmth of a bonfire and singing on the karaoke stage at four o'clock in the morning. Candles were lit, both in honor of the survivors, and in memory of those who had lost their lives. Maddie's team raised over $1,000.00. She was exceptionally proud of everyone on her team.

A few days later, Maddie had her eighth-grade graduation. Although she had missed a great deal of school over the past winter and spring months, her dedicated teacher made visits to the hospital to help Maddie keep up with her studies. Remarkably, Maddie managed to finish school with high marks and was graduating with her classmates and friends.

Like all young teens, she was extremely excited about graduation. We shopped for hours, committed to finding the perfect graduation dress. Together, we logged in what seemed like miles of shopping-mall corridors. We were both pleasantly exhausted from our wheelchair marathon. For me, it was worth every second as I witnessed the joy and light in her eyes when she finally found her perfect dress.

Maddie was very fatigued the day of her graduation. Yet, in spite of her obvious discomfort, she was exhilarated to be with her friends. It was a very special milestone. Preparing to see her graduate and receive her diploma was a dream come true. A year before, I could only pray and hope that this would happen.

At the graduation ceremony every student was given a single rose to give to their mother; I was honored and overwhelmed with pride and love when Maddie walked across the stage, and down the aisle towards me. She smiled and then whispered, "Thank you." All those months in the hospital, she managed her school work between treatments as best as she could. A few lessons a day, and her hard worked paid off. Her smile said it all; we had made a great team. I beamed with motherly pride over what she had accomplished.

All the students went off to a special graduation dance. Maddie was invited to join her friends in a limousine they had rented. I watched them drive off, the sound of laughter and delight lingering behind them. I kept my fingers crossed that Maddie would last a few hours and have the fun experience that she so deserved.

My brother Kevin decided that he should get the backyard ready for an after-graduation party in case Maddie was too tired and needed to come home to rest. Thank goodness for Uncle Kevin's foresight, because after the dance the entire class ended up at our house; a spontaneous and wonderful gift for Maddie. It was around 10 P.M., when Maddie arrived back with a few friends. She looked tired, but quickly rebounded when all her classmates started to unexpectedly arrive at the impromptu party. She rested on her lounge chair, playfully directing Uncle Kevin as he helped host the party.

Kevin gladly busied himself, getting the barbeque ready and building a small fire in the fire pit. Maddie's classmates quickly ditched their fancy gowns for their bathing suits and jumped in the pool. They swam under the moonlight, sat around the bonfire, and talked and joked until the sun came up.

I helped to serve the food and made sure to carefully hang up all the beautiful graduation dresses that had been quickly discarded on the floor in favor of swimsuits. Kevin and I enjoyed chaperoning the evening, and yes it was both wonderful and exhausting. We were all elated that Maddie had her friends surrounding her and she would always cherish the night of her very magical party. Later on, many of Maddie's classmates shared that it was the best night of their lives. I, too, had a wish… that it could be a moment frozen in time, never to be lost.

We knew there was still a long road ahead and I began to wonder if life would ever be "normal" again. The specialists had told us that Maddie would have to be monitored closely for the rest of her life. We began to appreciate each day and were thankful for the precious moments we shared. Nothing was ever taken for granted again.

14

I Can't Take It Anymore

In September, Maddie started ninth grade—three and a half months after her final treatment. High school can be intimidating for any young teen but for Maddie, it was a double whammy. Her hair had just started to grow back in after her chemo treatments, she had lost confidence in her physical body, and she still had difficulty focusing.

She complained of "chemo fog," a cognitive impairment that some cancer patients experience as a result of their chemotherapy treatments. Side effects included memory loss, difficulty focusing, and depression. Some patients recover quickly, for others it can take several years. Maddie knew school was going to be a challenge for her. She had trouble concentrating for any length of time, reading was difficult for her, and she was still physically weak. The use of her left arm was limited as a result of the surgery. Nevertheless, Maddie's goal was ambitious; she wanted to start the year off with a full load of courses, determined not to fall behind. She was also looking forward to the camaraderie of being in school; something that she had missed the year before.

Maddie attended St. Jean de Brebeuf High School. It was close to our home, and I could come pick her up quickly if she wasn't well. While many of her friends also chose to attend this local school, Maddie's two best friends were going to a school a little further away.

As she readied for the first day of school she pleaded with me, "Mom, please don't tell them I have cancer, okay? I don't want them to fuss over me." She hated having attention directed at her.

This was an unusually large high school and none of her classmates from grade school were in her new classes. It was important to her, at the beginning of the school year, to keep her battle with cancer private. She wanted to give students the opportunity to get to know her and focus on who she was as a person instead of her illness. She didn't want to be treated differently. However, we did tell the teachers because we needed their support, understanding, and vigilant eye.

Maddie had a physical education class and she tried to participate in the group exercises, which included running, volleyball, and general fitness activities. This was a struggle for her.

The last day of the first week of school, she came home upset and quite distraught. "Mom, they know. I don't know who told them, but I know that they know about my cancer."

"Maddie, how could you tell?"

"They were treating me differently today; they clapped really loud and cheered every time I did something simple, like touch the ball or try to do a push-up. I know they were just being supportive, but it was so embarrassing."

Maddie and I talked about how people were going to react to the news of her having cancer and that she needed to be aware that people would respond in different ways.

"Maddie, you need to expect that some people will respond with curiosity while others may feel awkward," I cautioned her.

"And some will just avoid me," she said sadly.

"Yes, Maddie, some won't know what to do or say, so they might avoid you," I agreed with her.

"It's frustrating, because I'm shy to begin with," she said. "I can't just walk up to people and make friends."

"Give it time Maddie, they will learn to love you," I said.

"Oh, you're my mom; you're supposed to say that." And off she went to her room.

Armed with this understanding, she felt better prepared to cope with issues as they came up.

We learned that not only were conversations challenging for her, but some people had difficulty including her in daily activities. Maddie's life had changed and she didn't seem to fit into the fast-paced world that people around her were living in. The truth was she *did* have limitations. We believed and hoped that she would overcome these short-term challenges.

On a few occasions she was invited to hang out at the mall, and once or twice to go Rollerblading. Although she appreciated the invitations, unfortunately she did not have the physical strength to keep up. Even getting to and from classes was beginning to be a challenge for her.

It was painful to watch her frustration. She would come home from school and curl up on the couch, tired and a little depressed.

There was nothing I could do. Maddie had always been a very popular girl and managed to fit into every group. I could see how deflated and sad she had become. She had lost so much already. The cancer truly affected every aspect of her life.

One day in October, I got a frantic call from her on my cell phone. I couldn't make out what she was saying because she was absolutely hysterical.

"I can't take it anymore!" she screamed in absolute panic into the phone.

I was in Thorold, Ontario, one hour away, picking up some new books for a library we were donating to the hospital. I dropped everything and sped back to Hamilton to pick her up from school. She wasn't there. She was so upset, that she had actually left by herself and walked all the way to our house a few miles away. I don't know how she physically had the strength to do that. She had always taken the bus, or I drove her.

When I got home I found her horribly distraught. She was shaking and crying. Through her tears, she tried to tell me what had happened. Between her sobs she explained that two girls at school had started bullying her. She couldn't understand why. She was still so upset and frightened that I could not calm her down.

They had laughed at her and teased her in the past but, on this particular day, they had gone too far. They had shoved her into a corner in the school hallway, blocked her path, and then started to mock her.

While her hair had finally started to back in after her chemotherapy, she still had to wear a bandana. They tormented her with questions: "Why do you look so weird? What is wrong with you?" they taunted.

She was devastated by their cruelty and so intimidated that she could not even respond. She was afraid of them.

She cried to me, "Isn't it bad enough that I have cancer? What have I done to deserve this?" Her face was red and swollen; however not from the harsh effects of chemo this time, but from the tears and heartbreak of being teased and mocked.

As a parent, the cancer diagnosis aside, I had never felt such rage. I felt angry and helpless at the same time. How could kids be so cruel?

I went to the school principal for help. I knew it was a great school, with an amazing reputation. The teachers and principal became involved immediately. They wanted to help, but Maddie would not tell them the names of the two girls.

With no threat of discipline to keep them in line, the girls continued with their intimidation tactics for months. They would laugh and smirk when Maddie faltered or dropped her books, and constantly whispered about her. She was always on edge when they were around, even out in public. Maddie started showing signs of losing her confidence. They almost succeeded in doing the one thing the cancer had not done, and that was destroy her spirit.

Then one day she must had decided she'd had enough. I was cleaning her room and found a crumpled up and torn piece of paper on the floor. Maddie had scribbled on it: *Screw the bitches. I'm not going to let them get to me. I'm going to focus on helping other people and ignore them.*

It was good to see that she was getting her feelings out, even if only on paper. It showed she was dealing with it better. She couldn't stop them from bothering her, but she would no longer allow them to have any power over her.

What made it such a hurtful experience for her was how aware she was of this issue; it had always bothered her to see anyone being bullied. She immediately wanted to step in and help.

Somehow, Maddie found the strength to put her bullying experience into perspective and began reaching out to others, offering them positive encouragement. From this experience, her empathy matured. She found peace knowing many teachers and students at her school cared. She wouldn't let two mean girls define her!

With Maddie in remission, I was able to go back to work full time. Every day I prayed that everything would be fine. Every three months, doctors closely monitored Maddie for a possible relapse; two down, one more to go.

15

The Beast Roars Again

Life settled down rather nicely and another enjoyable Christmas passed. We looked forward to a good long Ontario winter. We typically spent our winter weekends attending Derek's hockey games. We were his dedicated, enthusiastic cheering squad.

One very cold January morning, I was sitting at the kitchen table, reading and sipping my tea when Maddie walked over to me and said ever so quietly, "Mom . . . Mommy . . . my arm hurts."

For a minute, I thought I was daydreaming, having a flashback to the first time when Maddie came to me complaining that her arm hurt.

"Mom, this time it's my other arm." There was a sense of urgency and fear in her voice.

My mind, deep in another place, slowly tried to register what I was hearing, *Other arm . . . ?* I snapped out of my daze.

"Say that again, Maddie." I turned towards her.

"My other arm hurts. The pain is in my shoulder, too," she spoke with alarm.

"Darling, I'm sure it's going to be fine," I said, trying to mask my own panic. "I will call the doctor and set up an appointment. Don't worry, okay?" I was trying desperately to sound calmer than I felt.

I was frantic as we whisked ourselves back to the doctor's office. They seemed grim as they went about the task of setting up new tests: a biopsy of a suspected tumor in her right shoulder and a bone-marrow biopsy. It was so difficult to be patient.

Finally the call arrived and I went to the appointment alone because Maddie was in school. When I walked into the doctor's office, I had a sense of déjà vu; I had seen that look before. I knew I needed to sit down and brace myself for the news.

"Mrs. Babineau, we are sorry to tell you, the cancer has come back."

"That's impossible!" I stammered. "You put her through hell with the aggressive treatment. How could the cancer survive?"

"It's tricky . . . all it takes is one cell to start up again." he said, "We can only hope for the best; sometimes we don't get the results we want."

My mind was reeling. The cancer had spread to her right shoulder. How could this happen? All that chemotherapy, the pain from the surgery, weeks of radiation, long stretches of time away from friends. She had lost part of her childhood. Now, we were facing the monster again. Her body had not yet fully recovered from the previous battle. We had to start over again. What would the future hold?

I tried to calm my racing heart. Maddie was a trooper, I reminded myself. She beat it once already; I prayed she had the strength to do it again. "It isn't fair," I lamented. We'd been warned that if the disease returned, we would have a *real* fight ahead of us. Relapse. I needed to steel myself for another difficult stretch, and tell my brave daughter she had to slay the dragon again.

Our lives were turned upside-down—again. Maddie was readmitted to the hospital to treat the new arm pain and a fever. Once she was settled and resting comfortably in her room, I tip-toed out to a scheduled meeting with her doctor. I braced myself as I sat across from him, feeling very vulnerable.

He began to explain what her relapse meant. He expressed his concern, and the seriousness of the situation came through in his tone, as he carefully explained the limited options. I believe that he tried to convey this news as gently as possible—almost shielding me from its cold reality.

I sat there numb, the words piercing through my broken heart. He spoke of creating a palliative care team. I knew what a palliative care team was needed for; we had one when Stephen's health had gravely deteriorated. Their main focus is on improving quality of life, at end of life, for both the patient and the family.

Fighting the panic, I knew I had to focus on the facts while remaining hopeful. I couldn't fall apart now. We had to re-examine whether it was possible to beat this cancer. I assured the doctor we were not giving up. I tried to keep the fear at bay as we planned the next fight against the aggressive cancer that was ravaging Maddie's battered and frail body.

I went back to her room to break the news, but I froze outside the door. I didn't have the heart to tell her. I paced for an hour not wanting to crush her spirit. "How do you tell your child that her cancer is back?"

I knew I needed to be the one to give her the news, not the doctors. I finally found the courage to open the door to her room. She was sitting on her bed reading.

"Maddie, we need to talk."

"Sure Mom," she said, putting her book aside. I noticed it was *Macbeth*; must have been homework.

"I met with the doctors," I said carefully as I sat at the end of her bed.

"No!" she cried. I didn't have to say anything more, my face and voice said it all; she knew the answer.

"Maddie, it will be okay, we just have to do this again. One more time, okay?" I pleaded with her.

"Mom, don't tell me the cancer is back." her eyes pleading with me to say, " Maddie, everything is fine." But I couldn't.

"Maddie, I am so sorry, the doctor said sometimes a tiny cell gets away and the cancer can start up again. We are going to try a new chemotherapy drug. Hang in there, you're a fighter." I tried to summon up all the enthusiasm that I could manage.

"Mom, I don't want to, I'm tired of being sick," she said looking very defeated.

I wrapped my arms around her. "You can do this, you did it already. It will be over before you know it."

She turned away and buried her head in her pillow. I sat there, willing all her pain to transfer over to my body. I couldn't bear to see her looking so hopeless. God, I hated cancer!

I was painfully aware of how precious time was becoming, and how difficult the journey ahead would be. Thus started the rollercoaster ride: more hospital visits, new chemotherapy treatment, missed school, time away from friends and family—all with the hope this treatment would be the magic potion.

Maddie had just started to get her life back to normal, hanging out with her friends, going to a real school. Her brief remission had allowed her to have some normalcy. Now she was cruelly uprooted again.

The new chemotherapy drug was going to be administered over two sessions, after that a high-dose chemotherapy treatment followed by a stem cell transplant would be considered.

We once again packed our bags and returned to life in the hospital. Knowing her way around the hospital, Maddie bravely settled in.

16

Another Wish, Please!

A highlight for Maddie during this difficult time was the work in Africa. The Children's Wish Foundation had provided Craig's foundation with money in her name to build the school, and her wish had just recently been fulfilled: a small, brick, one-room classroom. The students wrote letters to her, thanking her for their precious gift of an education. They sent her pictures, too.

"It is perfect," Maddie said when she saw it. She was delighted to hear from the children and shared the letters she received with everyone on the ward. She couldn't wait for the mail to come. She would always greet me by asking the same question "Is there any mail for me?"

Craig Kielburger also sent her items from the places he travelled around the world. Maddie looked forward to these wonderful gifts; a book from Thailand, a scarf from Equador, and a necklace from Haiti. She had a special shelf for these precious keepsakes. She would search online to learn all she could about each country.

"I am going to all these places when I get better!" she proclaimed. It gave her hope. One morning, I brought her a care-package, a small box that had arrived in the morning mail. She jumped from her bed, delighted to receive it.

"For me?" she asked eagerly.

She opened it carefully, and ever so gently took out a round, brown ceramic bowl. It was a piggy bank, made in Africa. A handwritten note said, "Come and join us."

"Mom, I am going to get healthy and go to Africa one day and meet these beautiful children," she declared.

Very coyly, she held out her hand and said, "Do you have any spare change to help me get there?"

Maddie went around to everyone she knew asking for spare change. I could tell by the determined look on her face she was set on getting better and making this trip happen.

The difficult task of finding a cure continued. After much research, and consultations with various groups and doctors, we had come to the conclusion that Maddie would benefit from being cared for at Sick Kids Hospital in Toronto, where she could receive a stem cell transplant after the chemo treatment. Sick Kids Hospital was the only facility in the region that could perform this type of procedure. There was a chance that this high-dose chemotherapy treatment followed by a stem cell transplant (to aid her system in recovery from the chemo) might be the miracle she needed.

This was an aggressive form of treatment, and unfortunately had a very low success rate for her type of cancer. But, the alternative—to give up—was unthinkable. I explained to Maddie this was going to be another tough go. After the shock of the relapse set in, she was willing to endure whatever it took to beat her cancer.

We drove to Toronto for a meeting with the specialist who would be overseeing the stem- cell transplant. He explained the difficult process ahead of us, the protocol, and expected setbacks. He turned to Maddie and said gently, "Unfortunately Maddie, due to the side effects of the chemotherapy drug, it most likely will render you sterile."

"What do you mean?" Maddie asked confused.

"You probably will not be able to have children when you are older."

"No!" she gasped.

"Mommy, no!" She crumpled in her chair. She'd had enough heartache! She started to cry. Tears and retching sobs came out of her tiny body. I rushed to her side and wrapped my arms around her. This was cruel, she loved kids, she had dreamed of having children of her own. I held her and rocked her small body, trying to calm her.

She was much too young to have to face such consequences. "Mom, let me go," she sobbed, trying to pull away.

I didn't know what to do; I held her tighter.

"I don't want to stay here, I've had enough," she said pleading, I gently released her. She left the room with her head hanging low, her body looking beaten and defeated.

I was not able to spend one more minute in that room—the room where all her future dreams had just been snatched away from her. I followed behind her, not knowing how to help her or what I could say that would take her suffering away.

I followed her as she sat down at a bench in the hallway. I watched her for a moment, then I approached her as lovingly as I knew how.

"Maddie, are you okay, do you want to talk?" I asked her quietly.

"Mom, he said I won't be able to have children," she cried. She turned to me. "What am I doing all this for?" she asked desperately.

"Maddie, keep your hopes up okay? Don't give up. He said, 'might not', there is still a chance you can." We both knew I was grasping at straws.

"Mom, I'm really tired of all of this."

"Please Maddie, just hang in a little longer, okay? I think this stem cell transplant is the answer to getting you better."

She stared at me long and hard. The look she gave me will be forever emblazoned in my mind. For the first time I realized she really didn't believe me. It shook me to my core. I couldn't begin to imagine what was being processed in her mind, to understand what she was experiencing. I prayed that I was right, and that this treatment would work.

"Maddie, maybe we have to take it one day at a time, okay," I urged her.

"I guess," she said, and we held each other.

We returned to Hamilton and Maddie started her chemotherapy treatments, while the doctors in Toronto worked out the details of the chemo and stem cell transplant procedure. We were back to the familiar routine at McMasters Children's Hospital. Maddie and I never discussed the upcoming transplant or its possible consequences. After only a few days, Maddie started to come around, returning to her more playful and relaxed self.

One quiet afternoon, when there was very little happening at the hospital, and Maddie was resting comfortably, I took advantage of the down time and went home to spend some quality time with Derek. We went to a movie.

When I returned to the hospital, I opened the door to Maddie's room, and was immediately greeted by that "look". I hadn't seen it in a long time. It was a look that said "you've got to be kidding me," complete with eye-rolling and a determined expression. I smiled, knowing something was up. She was propped up on her hospital bed, loose papers spread across her lap, and she was using her computer on her bedside table. The remnants of her dinner were pushed to the side.

"It's not fair. I can't believe it!"

"What happened, Maddie?" I asked, curious by her passionate tone.

"We've got to do something," she cried out as if shocked by some tragic news.

She went on, words spilling forth at a rapid pace. "Do you know that many young girls cannot attend school because they have too many chores to attend to? They have to walk for miles and miles to fetch water for their families. I can build a school but they still can't go. That is so not fair!" She talked so fast I could barely keep up with her words.

"Maddie, slow down, explain."

Through a report she was reading about Africa, Maddie had discovered that many of the children, particularly the girls, were not attending school even when one was available. Many of them had the daily chore of fetching water, from a source some miles away. Sometimes they had to make that time-consuming and physically exhausting trip twice a day.

Maddie knew that without education, those wonderful children would have a very bleak future. "I don't want to feel ungrateful, but I wish I had wished for the wish of more wishes!" she said, easily handling her complex tongue-twister.

"But not for me!" she blurted. "More wishes so I could do more, build more schools and drinking wells, and make their lives better!"

She told me she had seen pictures of young children, as young as seven years old, carrying babies on their backs and they were not allowed to go to school. "Mom, I just couldn't imagine how a young child could handle all those responsibilities."

She reasoned, "If we build a well by the school, the children will never have to make that long walk again to the river and there will be no excuse for them not to go school."

She closed her eyes and puckered up her face, "I wish for more wishes!" she commanded out loud.

Nothing . . . so she said it again, even more dramatically, her eyes flashing and arms flailing. "I wish for more wishes!"

Still nothing.

She threw her hands in the air, laughed, and said, "Well *that* didn't work!"

"Mom," she said seriously, "I'm going to build a drinking well. How can we raise more money?"

"Well, I don't know, can you sing or dance for it?" I teased her.

"Very funny, let me think about it." And off she went down the hallway.

She came back about five minutes later and sat in front of me, a look of passion and pain intermingled on her face. "Seriously, if I really had one wish left, I would wish I could have children of my own one day."

Maddie took a breath. "But, that is not going to happen now," she said sadly. "I really want to help these children in Africa, I feel like they can, in a way, be my children. I can help them."

My heart skipped a beat, hearing her so courageously plan her future—finding a way to overcome her own heartache and disappointment.

"Can you help me find a way to raise money and do this, please?" she asked.

She convinced me that she wanted to use whatever precious energy she had left to raise money that would directly help the young children. These children had not only captured her heart, but she now had decided to mindfully adopt them as her own.

I felt such overwhelming pride. Her compassionate heart left me breathless, and through her actions she was teaching me a powerful lesson in selflessness.

"Yes, Maddie, I will help you." It was the least I could do. I swore to myself, I would move heaven and earth to ensure my daughter got her wish. With her big heart, there was no doubt the drinking well would be built.

17

Going to War

Before Maddie could start any fundraising efforts, we received the news that we would be going to Sick Kids Hospital for her stem cell transplant.

We had a few days to settle in before treatment started. She had her own small room; it was plain and barren. It was meant as a sort of holding space for a few days, and she would be moved to an isolation room after her treatment.

The procedure took place in a special area of the hospital. There were machines that filtered her blood and broke it down to harvest her stem cells. These healthy cells, untainted by the toxic treatment, would be saved. She would receive the healthy stem cells back as part of her recovery—after the high-dose chemotherapy.

The following day, June 28, 2006, was my birthday. I had almost forgotten it, but Maddie hadn't. Even though worried about her own upcoming treatment, she was able to make this day special for me. Ever resourceful, she used some hospital scrapbooking supplies she found lying around to make me a paper birthday cake, complete with paper candles. I could not imagine any place I would rather have been than right there by her side.

I spent each night in Maddie's hospital room. I also had a room at the Ronald McDonald House, a place created for out-of-town family members to stay while their child was being treated. I used it to quickly shower, or use the computer to briefly connect with the outside world. I felt isolated and lonely; I wished for the thousandth time that Stephen was there with me.

Derek stayed in Hamilton with his uncle Kevin during Maddie's treatment. Children under twelve years old were not allowed in the isolation room and he was only ten, so he could not visit his sister. Kevin would bring him to Toronto on weekends and Derek stayed in my room at the Ronald McDonald House. I would slip out of the hospital when I could and spend time with him. He was a hockey nut, so I made sure we took the time to visit the Hockey Hall of Fame.

The day of Maddie's high-dose chemotherapy, the nurse came into her room wearing protective clothing even more intimidating than that worn by the nurses during Maddie's previous rounds of chemo. I was extremely unnerved by the high level of protection they needed just to handle the radioactive drugs. What she wore looked like the protective gear an astronaut would wear in outer space, or like what I had worn in the military during my nuclear, biological, and chemical warfare training. It was clear, we were going to war. I couldn't imagine the damage this would do to Maddie, with the poison being absorbed throughout her system.

As I watched, I questioned myself again for the millionth time, *"Are we doing the right thing?"* I saw this as our only hope. Maddie had assured me that she trusted my judgment; she knew I only wanted what was best for her. I was trying to save her life. How I wished I could have taken her place.

The isolation room was intimidating, a high-level germ-free environment. Other than Maddie and the medical staff, I was the only one allowed in. I scrubbed before entering, and wore a gown, gloves, and mask. It was critical that we did not touch anything. When something fell to the floor, such as my book or sweater, it was scooped up and taken away to be sterilized.

Special clean air was pumped in. Because I was not allowed to bring in any food or drink, I stayed by her side except for brief moments when I went to get something to eat. A special team, familiar with the protocol, was assigned to Maddie's care.

Nothing up to this point, in all the close calls and emergency treatments, had prepared us for this part of her difficult journey. Maddie soon became very sick. She was in agony throughout her treatment. As the chemotherapy did its work, the side effects started. She struggled to breath, could not swallow, and developed blisters in her mouth. It was horrible to watch her as she suffered through the fevers and pain.

Her fingernails and toenails fell off. Her hair fell out again, including her eyelashes, and eyebrows. She lay listless on her hospital bed; she was frail and near death and there was nothing I could but hold her and surround her with my love. She had no energy to speak; and struggled to make it through each day.

There was such a sense of hopelessness. I was overwhelmed with the guilt of choosing to take this extreme measure to try to save her life. I was fist-clenching angry at the whole world for what was happening, and angry at myself because I could do nothing to stop it.

I was scared, terrified at what I was witnessing, and not knowing what more was to come. I would sit there for days watching her, numb with fear and guilt; because I had been the driving force behind the decision to choose this treatment.

For a month, I witnessed Maddie fight for her life. She somehow survived by what must have been sheer willpower. After a difficult four weeks, she was moved out of isolation to the step-down ward. In spite of this optimistic sign, she was not yet eating or drinking and was on high doses of morphine for the pain.

She finally received the stem cell replacement. The stem cells would help her rebound from the chemotherapy and return her health.

Once Maddie was stable, we were to return to McMaster Children's Hospital, where they would resume her care. After thirty-two long and difficult days, Maddie and I returned by ambulance to the isolation ward at McMaster. She was still receiving pain control (hydomorphone) and her nutrients by IV as she had gone for almost five weeks without eating or drinking anything.

She was pale and thin. It had been a while since we had seen her smiling face. The doctors were worried because she had been bedridden for so long. We needed to get her strong and healthy. Muscle atrophy and clots were a possibility. We worked towards getting her up walking, and encouraged her to drink sips of water. Her whole system had shut down as she fought hard to recover from the chemotherapy.

Maddie still required another surgery as well. It was to be done as soon as she was strong enough. We knew that time was critical. There must not be a long lapse between the chemo and getting the new tumor removed.

Despite what seemed dismal times, we were happy to be back in Hamilton; Maddie, Derek and I were together again. He could stay with her in her room and I got to steal moments away to watch his football practices.

Although, I had no choice, it was difficult not being there as much as I needed and wanted to be for Derek. It was amazing how at the tender age of ten he seemed to understand. He was genuinely appreciative of the time we were able to spend together and, more importantly, he loved having his big sister back in Hamilton.

At seven weeks post-stem cell transplant, Maddie was still unable to eat or drink. She underwent an endoscopy that revealed inflammation of the esophagus. She continued to suffer from extreme nausea and burning in her throat—all part of the healing process from the treatment.

It was necessary to insert a nasogastric tube so that we could get her off the TPN (nutrients given intravenously to replace food). Nasogastric intubation is a medical process involving the insertion of a plastic tube through the nose, past the throat, and down into the stomach. Once we were able to get her morphine and other meds through her NG tube, she would no longer need to stay in the hospital; the hope was to bring her home.

Throughout this time, Maddie was going to physiotherapy and, although she tended to fatigue when she walked even a short distance, her spirits were actually good. The doctors promised her that if she was able take in her nutrients and keep them down for sixteen hours, they would give her permission to leave on an eight-hour pass.

18

For Sale

*W*e had been back in Hamilton for two weeks. Finally, Maddie showed some renewed energy and her spirits were lifting. One day, she said, "Mom, we need to raise money for the well in Africa, remember. How can we do it?"

I wasn't too sure. With Maddie spending all of her time in the hospital, the options seemed pretty limited. We put our heads together; what could we do?

One thing she liked to do with her down time was surf the Web on her computer. Maybe she could find something online? She was familiar with eBay, a site where people can buy and sell items online. Maddie found a store selling beautiful jewelry—bracelets and earrings—for a great price if you bought them in bulk. I told her I would be pay for them, and then she could resell them to friends and family, making money that way.

Maddie placed an order for 200 beautiful beaded bracelets and 100 necklaces and earrings, then she waited excitedly for her order to come in. She researched how much she should charge, and spent her time making up posters that would be ready for display when the items arrived.

Two weeks later they came; I brought the packages straight to the hospital. Maddie took delight in carefully opening the package and sorting through all the wonderful jewelry. They were wrapped in bubble wrap, the beautiful colors coming through. She spread everything out on her hospital bed, a colorful mosaic of blue, red, orange—every color of bead imaginable. They were nicer than she had hoped for. Excitedly she went about setting up shop.

Maddie quickly became a young entrepreneur. She had a mini storefront set up in her hospital room. She had foam boards that she poked holes in to display the jewelry. She lined her hospital windowsill with them. They were on her bed, her dresser, her bedside table. The word got out through the nurses and staff. Maddie made signs up that read: "For Africa –Necklaces $10, Bracelets $5, Earring $5. Thank YOU!"

Doctors and nurses showed up at Maddie's bedside, and instead of poking and prodding her, they laughed, chitchatted and bought jewelry from her. She had a great time selling to everyone who came by. It was fun watching everyone fuss over how beautiful the jewelry pieces were.

All the proceeds went to Maddie's African well project. It was a win-win opportunity for everyone; they purchased beautiful jewelry at a great price and they were helping to raise money for a wonderful cause.

Maddie's fifteenth birthday was on the horizon, Thursday, August 24, 2006. She had been fighting cancer since she was diagnosed at the young age of twelve. Her goal was to make it home for her birthday, if only for a few hours. A few hours that would mean the world to her.

On the morning of Maddie's birthday, she still was not eating, and this meant she had not met the medical requirements that would allow her to go home. Nevertheless, the doctors gave into our pleading, and let me take her home. We had a four-hour pass to celebrate her birthday.

I had asked family and friends to come by the house during those four hours, and those who weren't able to come sent Maddie e-mails and cards, and left her beautiful phone messages. It really made her day special. Forty people joined us at the house to share in the celebration which, somehow, I was able to keep a surprise.

Maddie was flustered and excited by all of the attention. She was smiling, and even her eyes were shining and bright against her pale skin as she walked through the door and was greeted by the crowd of well-wishers. I hadn't seen her like this in ages; it was so nice to witness.

"Hello everyone," she said. "Thanks for coming for my birthday." She hugged her aunts and uncle, friends and neighbors. She sat in her favorite chair by the window, holding court with Winston by her side. She couldn't eat, but she fussed over her friends making sure they all ate the food and wonderful birthday cake. This celebration was the best medicine anyone could prescribe for her.

Just before we returned to the hospital, a wonderful young girl named Holly came up to Maddie. "I have something for you," she said shyly.

"What is it?" Maddie asked.

"It's a check for the money I made selling lemonade to raise money for your project in Africa." She presented a check to Maddie for $120.00.

Maddie's eyes grew wide and a smile broke out on her face. She was thrilled by this wonderful gesture and warmed by the knowledge that someone had been moved to take action for her cause. "Thank you so very much Holly," she said sincerely, giving her a hug.

In the car on the way back to the hospital, Maddie excitedly said, "Mom, this is so amazing. That little girl helped me. She raised money for the well!" She turned to me and continued, "I know we can do this, soon we will have enough money to build a well for the children in my school." Maddie was clearly determined and confident that others would help.

At the end of September, Maddie was finally released from the hospital with the hopes she'd be able to stay home until the surgery. But she was home only a few days, when on a Thursday she started to experience a new type of pain that got increasingly worse as the day wore on. She said it was an unbelievable pain that she had never experienced before. In light of what she had already gone through, I knew it must be something serious.

We went into the hospital Friday morning and Maddie was diagnosed with shingles, caused by the same virus as chickenpox. Maddie was moved to isolation, and we were told that her surgery on the fourth would have to be postponed by two weeks, although they couldn't set an exact date.

Maddie was understandably frustrated. She felt as though she could never escape the hospital. The smell of disinfectant permeated her clothes—even long after we left. The hurried and stressed looks on the nurses, the crying of young children and the constant poking and prodding she received daily was beginning to wear on her. When feeling worn down, she would say, "Mom, I hate it here! I can't wait to get out." It took a week to get the shingles under control. Finally, the doctors were comfortable with sending her home.

19

Believe in Magic

During this time friends and family had been planning a fundraiser for our family called Moving Mountains for Maddie. The event was planned for the Saturday after Maddie returned from the hospital. We'd been so afraid that maybe Maddie wouldn't be able to attend.

Maddie was so relieved to be home. We were looking forward to the event. I saw a spark in her eye that I hadn't seen in a long, long time.

It was a very special evening. The money raised would offset the loss of my wages from not being able to work, and to pay for the many spiraling costs including gas, parking, supplements and medical items for the home. The list was long.

Maddie was restless with anticipation the night before the party, looking forward to a special celebration. She spent Saturday after-noon getting ready for the big night. She was all smiles as she and her girlfriend Vicki picked out their clothes. The banquet hall was only a block away so we pushed Maddie over in her wheelchair.

The ballroom was beautifully decorated with hundreds of purple balloons—Maddie's favorite color. We entered the building and were greeted by hundreds of Maddie's family, friends and supporters. It was standing-room only.

It warmed her heart to have such support from the community, friends and even strangers. She stood at the front door greeting every-one, welcoming them in.

A woman who lived in the area and who was originally from Af-rica had learned about Maddie and how she had used her wish from the Children's Wish Foundation to build a school in Africa . When the woman heard about the fundraiser, she had asked if she could attend the event and help out. She was dressed beautifully in her colorful native clothing. She set up a table with items from her homeland for people to purchase; the money would be going to Maddie's cause.

When Maddie arrived, the woman rushed over and gave her a big hug and told Maddie about her experiences back home. Maddie glowed while they chatted, bombarding the woman with so many questions about Africa. She felt as though it was almost a firsthand experience to connect in some way with the village people who meant so much to her.

There was a band, food and a silent auction for bidding on delightful items. People mingled, enjoying the sense of community and celebration of life. There was even a breathtaking magic show made all the more special because the illusionist, Brian Michaels, was himself a survivor, having undergone a double-lung transplant only three months earlier. He knew what Maddie was going through and he graciously volunteered to help make our night very special.

Toward the end of his performance, Brian called Maddie up to the stage. We all held our breath as we watched her. She slowly pulled herself out of her wheelchair.

Michael bent down toward and whispered, "Maddie, you have to believe in magic." Then a rose magically appeared between his fingers.

"This is for you." He extended a beautiful red rose to her.

She reached up and took the flower in her slender fingers and turned to face us with a beautiful smile. The hall exploded with cheers and Maddie got a standing ovation.

It was a moving moment for everyone there; two heroes on the stage, side by side, Maddie and Brian. We were grateful to witness their courage, and to be thankful for our lives, both the highs and the lows. We felt connected; it was a magical night.

I felt very blessed. My heart was filled with appreciation and my spirits were raised. All of this reinforced my belief that, with all of this loving support, Maddie would make it.

20

Boomerang Wish

Maddie's surgery had finally been scheduled for October 27, 2006, at 8:00 A.M. She woke up that morning to the bustling of hospital staff prepping her to go the operating room. As I accompanied her down the hallway, I vowed to stay with her till they had sedated her completely, just like the last time.

On the operating table, she turned to me and said, "I like the peaceful feeling of drifting off to sleep." She smiled as the anesthetic took effect. "Night, night Mom, I love you." And out she went.

In order to remove the tumor this time, the surgeon had to replace Maddie's right scapula and the bone in her arm. In its place she would receive a prosthetic shoulder and arm.

Her first surgery had already damaged the nerves and affected the range of motion in her left arm. Now both arms would have limited movement.

Hours later, when the surgeons finally wheeled Maddie out, I jumped up from my seat and leaned in to her on the gurney. "How are you darling?" I whispered.

She opened her eyes for a brief moment, then drifted back to sleep. Her arm was carefully bandaged.

After the nurses wheeled Maddie back to her room, they quickly began to set up the equipment for pain management. The process was all too familiar: an epidural along with a morphine patch, and hourly hydromorphone (pain medicine). As with the first surgery, Maddie was still quite uncomfortable, nauseated, throwing up, and exhausted.

We arrived home on November 9, hoping this time would be for good. I arranged for Maddie to get physiotherapy at home. She regained some range of motion, but she was still not able to move her arm on its own.

Maddie was now in the fifth month after the stem cell transplant and her appetite was slowly returning. She continued to use the feeding pump nightly to ensure she got all the nutrients she needed for her body to sustain itself.

Pain was still an ongoing issue that she dealt with as best she could. She complained sometimes that it felt like her prosthetic shoulder was separating; an X-ray confirmed that it was fine. The staples were taken out. Her surgeon did an amazing job and the incision healed well.

Our living room morphed into Maddie's bedroom. We stationed her bed, feeding pump and medical supplies in here and it looked like a field hospital. We homeschooled Maddie through this recovery time; it was not too much of a course load, just two credits per semester.

She had a wonderful relationship with her teacher Mrs. Cil Carducci. Maddie worked hard to complete her assignments and keep up with her schoolmates. During one of Mrs. Carducci's visits, Maddie excitedly told her that she wanted to do something for Derek. She was going to paint his room.

"What do you want it to look like Maddie?" asked Mrs. Carducci.

"I want to paint it the color of the Ottawa Senators hockey team," she said excitedly.

"So, you like hockey?"

"Yes, our whole family loves hockey! Especially the Ottawa Senators because we were born there," Maddie said. "And I *love* Wade Redden," she gushed.

"You like Wayne who?" Mrs. Carducci asked.

"Wade . . . Wade Redden. I have a crush on him!" Maddie declared.

They resumed their lesson. A few minutes later, Maddie winced in pain, "Mom, can I have some more morphine please?"

"You can't yet, you just had some," I replied from the kitchen.

"Maddie do you want a break?" asked Mrs. Carducci, seeing that Maddie was in extreme discomfort.

"No, that's okay, let's keep working." She smiled weakly.

Before she left that day, Mrs. Carducci noted to me that she had never seen Maddie gush over someone like she had over Wade. It had been wonderful to see her behave like a typical teen, smitten with her favorite sports hero. She told me that her niece was in Ottawa and knew one of the players on the team. Maybe, they could work something out and have Wade give Maddie a call. Mrs. Carducci phoned me later that evening and told me it was all set, and to be on the lookout for a phone call for Maddie the next day.

Unfortunately, we had to go to the hospital for testing the next day. When we returned, I saw that there were five missed calls on the phone. My heart sank. I hope he calls back, I prayed. I waited anxiously all evening for the phone to ring again.

Finally, an unknown number came up on the phone, it must be him.

I grabbed it, and passed it to Maddie.

"Hello," she said.

"Hello Maddie, how are you?" the person on the other end asked.

"Who is this?" she shyly asked.

"It's Wade Redden."

"No, it's not!" she said, looking at me as if to say, "Is this a trick?" I nodded and mouthed, "No, it's really him."

"Oh, hello," she said, her eye wide with surprised.

They talked for a while. I could only hear her end of the conversation. Lots of "uh"… "Uh hums" and lots of girlish giggling. I had never seen her like this before and it was a treat.

When she eventually hung up the phone she turned to me and said, "Mom, you won't believe it, Wade invited us, the whole family, to a hockey game. He's playing in Buffalo next week. It's only an hour away! Please, please can we go, please?"

"Of course, we can." I was delighted by this unexpected gift for Maddie. How could we possibly turn it down? I then told Maddie how Mrs. Carducci had arranged the whole thing. When her teacher arrived the following day, before she had time to take her coat off, Maddie blurted, "Mrs. Carducci thank you so much for getting me the opportunity to meet Wade Redden."

"Maddie, it was my pleasure. You work so hard, it will be a wonderful experience for you. Have fun!" Mrs. Carducci said.

"But how did you know?" Maddie asked seriously.

"Know what?" Mrs. Carducci asked.

"How did you know that was my wish?" exclaimed Maddie.

"What do you mean Maddie?

"If I hadn't given my wish away, I would have asked to meet Wade. That was my original wish, but then I thought about the children in Africa, and how they needed my wish more! I really never thought I would ever meet Wade, but now I am. Oh thank you so much!" She reached over and gave her a big hug.

"Really Maddie, I had no idea," Mrs. Carducci responded, hugging her back.

I watched Mrs. Carducci's face change, and tears fill her eyes. She tried to hide it by smiling and looking away. Much later she told me that she struggled to compose herself until she had gotten back in her car, where she broke down crying. She cried her heart out for the young girl who had the heart of a lioness, and who she had grown to love so much. The girl who had to take morphine like candies, who never complained when she had to do her homework. The girl who always wanted to please her mother, and who was beyond generous with her limited energy.

She was humbled that she was the one entrusted to help start the amazing chain of events designed to grant a wish to this extraordinary girl; the wish that she had given up for others. Amazingly, Maddie's wish made its way back to her and it was one of the most powerful and moving lessons of her life.

21

Escape to Africa, Canada

A follow-up appointment with Maddie's surgeon on November 19 left me feeling optimistic. He told us he felt that the surgery had gone extremely well. Her prosthetic limb was fitting perfectly. Her bone marrow results were normal. They had been able to get a clear margin around the tumor, which meant that Maddie did not have to endure any additional radiation.

Now, we needed to focus on building her strength and continuing rigorous physiotherapy to gain as much use of her arm as possible. The next hurdle was to concentrate on catching up on her studies so she could actually attend school the next semester.

The day after receiving the wonderful news that she wouldn't require further radiation, Maddie graced the cover of the *Hamilton Spectator*. It was November 20, National Child Day in Canada. Maddie was being celebrated along with three other local young people as making a difference in the world. The article was titled "The Power of One—Children Changing the World." Maddie had been nominated by a teacher at school, not just because she had given her wish away, but because she was still continually fundraising to build a drinking well in Africa, all while battling cancer.

A reporter called the house, asking if he could do a story on Maddie. I held the phone out. "Maddie, a reporter wants to interview you."

She pushed it away. "No way, Mom," she said, all flustered.

I covered the phone with my hand so the reporter could not hear us.

"Maddie . . . take it." I extended the phone to her again.

"No way, I don't know what to say," she pushed it back.

"Hurry before he hangs up," I said

"It makes me nervous to talk."

"That's okay, this interview will help others understand what you are doing and I bet tons of people will help you with your drinking well, does that sound good?" I asked.

"Okay," she said, taking the phone. Within two minutes she had relaxed, was bantering playfully with the reporter, laughing, and easily sharing with him her vision for the world. She was so positive and the interview was a powerful one. I realized my daughter was finding her voice in a most amazing way. Her confidence was growing; she was becoming the person she was destined to be.

December 9, 2006, was a very special day for Maddie. Craig Kielburger was coming to Hamilton. He was the keynote speaker for the YMCA Peace Medal breakfast. She was going to join him there and sell her jewelry at the event.

She got up early that morning and fussed like any young girl would when she's about to finally meet one of her heroes and mentors in person.

"What should I wear?" she asked all flustered as she got ready for the big day. Panic was setting in. "Nothing fits. Mom, help me!" She had a pile of clothes all over her bedroom floor. "Where is my wig, I can't go without it," Maddie wailed.

"It's in the bathroom," I said, grabbing it as I passed by. "Here you go." Finally, she was happy; she was dressed in jeans, a top and sweater, and off we went.

Maddie was determined to work by Craig's side with his organization when she got better. Today, she would do just that. I helped her pack up all her jewelry, her hand-painted signs and her display boards. We placed all of it in a suitcase and I loaded it into the van.

I helped Maddie into the vehicle and we rushed off to the event that was being held at a very nice hotel. Maddie was greeted by the event planners and given a table to set up. She looked so cute and businesslike as she set about displaying the jewelry.

She looked around at all the people and excitedly said, "Mom, I think we are going to make a ton of money." This was much better than selling out of her hospital bed.

People surrounded Maddie at her table; she madly tried to sell to as many people as she could. Half the table was sold out when we all were asked to go inside to listen to the guest speaker, Craig Kielburger. I helped Maddie inside. She was holding onto her right arm; she had been working hard and probably overused it. She didn't complain; she was too excited to be there. She sat at a front table mesmerized by Craig, following his every word.

Escape to Africa, Canada

As I looked at Craig on stage and at Maddie sitting at the table to his left, I remembered back to two years earlier, when Maddie had first been diagnosed with cancer, lying frail in her hospital bed watching a documentary on TV about this young man that she had never met. She had been inspired by what he had accomplished. Now here they were together, both changing the world with their passion to help others. I felt extraordinary pride for both of them.

After the event, Craig gave Maddie a gift. She opened it, and her mouth dropped open; it was a Maasai warrior necklace from Africa; an exquisite beautiful blue, orange and red beaded necklace that held great significance. Maddie was now a decorated warrior.

We embraced Christmas and New Years as best we could. Maddie was hospitalized a few times, still struggling with nausea, pain and general weakness. Her G-tube was plugged and she had to undergo surgery to replace it.

Instead of getting better and stronger, she continued to get weaker and sicker. The doctors met with me and told me they suspected the cancer was back for the third time. I didn't dare tell Maddie until we knew for sure. Holding onto that dark secret was killing me.

Our family needed a break from all this misery, away from here. Maddie deserved to enjoy every day she had, so I searched for some-place fun and affordable that we could go. Knowing that time was precious, I wanted Maddie to see everything, do everything at lightning speed—explore, taste all there was in life, and do it now. Money was tight, but I didn't want any regrets.

I noticed a special on the Internet for a hotel stay at the Fantasyl-and Hotel in the West Edmonton Mall in Edmonton, Alberta. West Jet Airlines had given us a complimentary flight credit and we could use it for this trip.

The hotel had specialty themed rooms: Hollywood Night, Roman, Western—and African! Maddie might never make it to Africa, but at least I could take her somewhere to get a taste of what it might really feel like to be there—even if it was only a decorated hotel room.

When I explained my family situation to the reservation clerk, she offered us a free upgrade to the African suite. I was grateful for her generosity. With the free trip and upgrade, we could actually afford to go. I could hardly wait to share the news with my kids.

I gathered Maddie, Kevin and Derek in the kitchen. "I have great news," I exclaimed. "We are going on a trip."

"Maddie, I would love to send you to Africa, but it's just not possible. I have booked the next best thing. We are going to the West Edmonton Mall and staying at the Fantasyland Hotel, in a luxury African-themed room."

"Yes!!!" Maddie and Derek shrieked in unison. They were ecstatic.

We left on the January 13. Fortunately, the flight was direct from Toronto to Edmonton, and Maddie was able to rest comfortably. We checked into the hotel and it was even better than the pictures we saw. Our room was stunning, with a beautiful, colored African motif on the walls of Maasai warriors, lions and elephants. There was a four-person waterfall Jacuzzi, leopard flooring, drapes and bedding. There was a set of bunk beds in a safari setting. It was as close to Africa as we could get. We all loved it.

The mall was huge, so the staff provided Maddie with a wheelchair to get around. They were extremely accommodating and friendly, and also gave Maddie free passes for the many attractions. We made our way around the mall, taking in all of the sights.

There was so much to see, from viewing the replica of Christopher Columbus's flagship, the Santa Maria, situated in the middle of the mall, to mini golfing, to visiting the penguins. The mall offered everything you could imagine: a water park, indoor carnival, rollercoaster, and a skating rink.

Maddie was only able to stay up for short periods of time. When she needed a break, Kevin and Derek would go off and explore while Maddie and I rested in our wonderful African room. She would lie in the bed, looking so tiny. I would wrap a blanket around her and she would curl up in my arms. She would look out at the African wildlife scene painted so vibrantly on the walls; then she would close her eyes and imagine herself there. "Someday Mom, we will go," she said. "We will play with the children, and I will teach English in their classroom."

"Yes Maddie. One day, we will go," I promised. I enjoyed these moments—planning her future, and praying it would be there for her, and that I would always be able to keep her safe.

While exploring the mall, we discovered the ice-skating rink. Maddie really wanted to skate around it, even if it was only once. She had learned to skate as a child on Ottawa's Rideau Canal. I went to the kiosk to rent both of us skates. The young attendant took my money and handed me the two pairs of skates. I put Maddie's skates on her and she stood up from her wheelchair, ready to hit the ice. I hadn't noticed how odd this must have looked to the young man.

Suddenly, another man ran over to us, frantically waving a piece of paper. He wanted me to sign a waiver declaring that if Maddie was injured we would not sue. Maddie laughed when she realized how strange it must have seemed to them, to see her miraculously get out of her wheelchair and not only be able to walk, but also skate.

We returned home to Hamilton, feeling rested and happy. Maddie prepared for the new semester, determined to not be homeschooled again. "Mom, I feel better," she pleaded. "I want to go to Vicki and Danielle's school."

"But it's so far away," I countered. "Why don't you stay at your old school?"

"Mom, I like my old school, it's just because I miss Vicki and Danielle and I really want to hang out with them. If I can go to their school, then at least I can see them more often."

I knew every day was special and I wanted Maddie to enjoy herself as much as she could, so I allowed her to switch schools. I would drive the extra distance. I would do anything for her.

When the semester began in February, Maddie started her new school with her friends by her side, showing her around. Because her story had been in the paper, all the students at the school knew a great deal about her and they willingly embraced being friends and helping her.

"Hey Maddie, how are you?" they greeted her as she walked down the halls. She was in awe that they knew who she was and all the good work she had been doing. She received high- fives in the hallway; everyone smiled at her and her confidence soared. Selling her jewelry in the hospital and events like the one with Craig, and being interviewed, had really re-built her self-esteem. Although shy, she had a mannerism that was confident and earnest. She was excited to be back at school with friends her own age.

Maddie continued to raise money for Free the Children, she was interviewed on TV and even started a website to promote her work, called the MAD Project *(maddieswishproject.com)*.

22

The Promise

Barely a month after returning to school, on March 5, 2007, bad news reared its ugly head again. The doctors confirmed my worst fears. The cancer was back and it was relentless and spreading. I started calling every medical center in the world that had any interest in medical trials for Ewing's sarcoma. I needed to find Maddie a cure. I had to save her. I was frantic and desperate.

"Please," I begged them over the phone, "Give us one more chance. Give us something that could save her."

Most of the people I spoke with were very kind but they could not offer us a solution or hope. At one medical center, the doctor kindly told me, "Stay home, keep your daughter as comfortable as possible and simply love her."

Maddie had fought hard in the past. She wouldn't give up, and I refused to give up on her. I contacted the medical team from Sick Kid's Hospital in Toronto. I needed to find an alternative treatment. They agreed to meet with us. We made the decision to transfer Maddie from McMaster Children's Hospital to Sick Kids Hospital. She would be under their care. The time to get from home to hospital was around an hour; it seemed manageable.

Maddie underwent further testing and the doctors created a new treatment plan. The transition was smooth; Maddie had been there for her stem cell transplant and was familiar with the hospital.

Credit Valley Hospital in Mississauga was the satellite hospital for Sick Kids (A satellite hospital is one that locally provides certain aspects of a child's cancer care.). It was half an hour closer, making the commute easier on Maddie. This is where she would go for blood work, transfusions, and updates in between her treatments at Sick Kids.

With the cancer now back for the third time, doctors told us Maddie's treatment was more to help stop the growth of the tumors, so that she would be comfortable. They didn't say it in so many words, but it seemed a cure no longer seemed possible.

The thought of having to talk to Maddie about death terrorized me. I approached the medical staff for guidance. They were in favor of talking to Maddie about the possibility of her dying. I had always resisted. I never wanted to imagine this as even a remote possibility. I didn't want to give up, and I didn't want to scare her. Yet, I realized Maddie might be worried about dying, that she might have questions too. I agreed that if Maddie ever wanted to talk about it, I would have that difficult conversation with her.

That day arrived. It was a day without treatment. We were using this time to just hang out together, grateful to be home. Maddie walked into the living room, "Come sit with me," she said. She had just gotten back from visiting her best friend Vicki, who lived across the street. I could see that something was weighing heavily on her mind.

"I want to talk to you about something important." she said. She held her hand out to me, waving. "Come sit."

Smiling, I wandered over and plopped down beside her on the couch. I wasn't prepared for what came next. She looked at me; her intense blue eyes piercing right into mine. She looked so brave. She was wearing her "Poopiest of Days" T-shirt. Her jeans fitted loosely, legs curled under her. Her hair had just started to grow back in again, soft as a feather.

"Mommy, promise me something," she said seriously.

"Sure Maddie, anything for you," I responded.

"Promise me, you'll be happy . . . after I'm gone," she said.

She took a slow breath and released the words, "I'm not afraid to die."

I opened my mouth, wanting to interrupt what I was hearing. She raised her hand, as if to say, "Please wait, I need to say this, it is important."

"I'm more afraid for you and Derek than myself." She spoke with deep concern, a sense of profound purpose and urgency.

Her words hit me like a lightning bolt; it was an unexpected, life-altering moment. I wanted to flee the room. I wanted to argue, I wanted to deny all of it, but instead I sat calmly, understanding she needed to read my eyes. I held my gaze with hers. I nodded my head, slowly.

I wanted to speak, but the words eluded me.

Maddie went on, encouraging me, "Derek deserves to be happy and he needs a mom who is happy too."

She looked at me intently and repeated her heartfelt request,

The Promise

"Mommy, promise me you will be happy."

In barely a whisper, I responded, "Okay Maddie. Yes, I promise."

She knew the pain I felt; she wanted to lessen it somehow. She smiled a faint smile, and hugged me as if to say, "It will all be okay."

I made a promise to her that day, but I didn't believe I would ever be able to keep it. The pledge seemed such a burden—an impossible task. However, my desire to keep that promise would become the driving force that got me through my darkest days.

I watched her walk slowly down the hall to her brother's room and knock on his door. She took Derek outside and had a long talk with him; she was trying to pack in a lifetime of sister-brother bonding. She talked to him about life—her life—and all the knowledge she had gained. She imparted her special words to him. "Be good. Stay in school. Don't do drugs. Take care of Mommy, she needs you." It was a lifetime of lessons in a passionate ten-minute conversation. They came back in; arm in arm. It was obvious how much they adored one another.

Maddie continued with her task. She got on the phone and called her Uncle Kevin and had that heartfelt talk with him too. I don't know what they spoke about; it was between her and her Funcle.

It was an incredible and humbling experience. Her insight was flawless. What she did for us was amazing. In her own innocent and sincere approach she paved the way for us to be able to cope with what was to come. She secured our healing.

She let us know that she was satisfied with her life; she had experienced the love of two parents, she had a brother who was perfect in her eyes, and she was loved by her family and friends. She was grateful and felt fulfilled that she was able to make a difference in the world.

Her message for us was to understand that we did not need to suffer; it is a choice and there is a way out by accepting the things we cannot change. We need to live passionately even though there are no guarantees. We must celebrate the good, overcome the bad, and accept the unchangeable parts of life.

She made me promise to accept these beliefs, and embracing them would help me to keep my promise to be happy

23

Maddie Embraces Her Dream

Maddie knew that her time was precious and she wanted to use it wisely. This was a time to celebrate her charity work and get the word out so others would join in her efforts.

Maddie was surprised to learn that she had won Ontario Junior Citizen of the Year. Her previous school, St. Jean de Brebeuf High School, had proudly nominated her for her work in Africa. The awards dinner would be in Niagara Falls, Ontario, in April.

Niagara Falls was one of Maddie's favorite places in the world. We were immediately excited by this turn of events and the whole family proudly attended. Returning to that familiar paradise, with its breathtaking views of Niagara Falls, conjured up many memories for us. Before Maddie was diagnosed, we often drove drive the forty-five minutes to see the falls, watch the spectacular fireworks, visit the museums and arcades, and go on the amusement park rides.

At the ceremony, Maddie met the other twelve teen recipients from across Ontario who received the same award, and learned what good work they were doing. It was really empowering for her to see how others made a difference in the world, a few of them had to overcome obstacles just like she had. There were arrangements for them to go sightseeing and enjoy the town, but Maddie was not well enough to join them. She stayed back and rested at the hotel.

For the awards banquet, there was an official sit-down dinner. The sound of bagpipes announced each recipient's entrance to the dinner and the certificates were awarded by the Lieutenant Governor of Ontario, James K. Bartleman.

In spite of her fatigue, the experience of being with all these other inspirational teens, made Maddie more determined to work tirelessly on her project to help the beautiful children in Africa. She and her friends brought new fundraising initiatives to school. Even though she was missing a lot of class due to her treatment, on the days she was there, she worked feverishly for her cause.

The local news channel featured her piece the night she won her award in Niagara Falls. The media attention brought her story into the spotlight; everyone stopped her in the hallways: "Congratulations Maddie," "Way to go girl!" "How can I help?" they all asked.

Maddie came home one day flushed with excitement. "Mom, they get it. They really want to help me. I can't believe how kind everyone is." She looked exhausted but the shining light in her eyes seemed to camouflage her fatigue. She was thrilled that friends and classmates actively worked to raise the money she needed to build her well in Africa.

Her high school went all out. They were passionate about Maddie and her cause and they had a variety of events—all tremendous successes. Her principal said that the students had never put such an effort into anything else or raised as much money for one cause before.

Maddie was asked to come to the school assembly to receive the check for her drinking well in Africa. At the beginning of this project she estimated needing $6,500. She had earned about $1,000 so far with her jewelry sales. She was excited about the presentation, but she worried she might faint from nerves. She still didn't like it when all the attention was on her. She poked me and whispered, "Mom, what should I say? I don't have a speech," she asked frantically.

I quickly coached her, "Just say 'thank you' and accept the check." That's all she needed to say. They knew how important this cause was to her, and they knew why.

The principal called her name, "Come on up, Maddie, and accept this check."

Maddie walked shyly to the front of the auditorium, chewing nervously on her fingernails. Despite her trepidation, her glowing face and sparkling eyes exuded the joy she felt.

The principal announced that St. Thomas More raised $10,000 for the drinking well through different fundraising activities! Maddie was blown away.

"Maddie you are an inspiration to us all." the principal said. He walked over and presented her with the check "Would you like to say something?" he asked, handing her the microphone.

I held my breath. There were hundreds of students in the auditorium. All eyes were on her and you could hear a pin drop.

Maddie took the microphone and held it loosely in her hand, as if she was afraid to really take hold of it. She giggled and blushed, looked at the ground, shuffled her feet, then, taking a big breath, she looked out at the audience, eyes wide. Although you could see the nervousness, what came through more clearly was her pure gratitude for what they did for her cause.

The energy in that auditorium was palpable. She hesitated, knowing she had everyone's attention. She was barely audible but she gave a humble and passionate, "Thank you." They exploded to their feet, cheering. A standing ovation!

Maddie grinned from ear to ear, she stood straighter and was flushed with renewed confidence. The positive good wishes aimed at her strengthened her spirit; you could see it in her physical reaction. As I gazed at her, I couldn't comprehend how cancer cells could live in a body so full of love and hope.

St. Jean de Brebeuf and St. Thomas More High Schools continued their fundraising efforts. They held carnivals, moustache-growing contests (Moustaches for Maddie), and created a wishing well to toss coins into. Students from other schools became involved. Tens of thousands of dollars came in. Maddie was in her glory; with their support she realized there was even more she could do.

At the end of April, she came home from school all excited. "Mom, we can't stop now, this is amazing. I am going to contact Craig and see what else we can do; I think we can build a whole village." This idea lifted her spirits as she braced herself for her next round of chemotherapy.

A week later, fatigued from all her good work and her treatments, Maddie was admitted to the Credit Valley Hospital. Her body temperature was raging and I was worried because the medical staff couldn't break the fever. After two days, they finally got it to come down a bit.

Maddie and her two best friends had missed exchanging Christmas gifts that year. Our lives had been too full of hospital visits and treatments for such carefree celebrations. On May 7, I was finally able to get her a temporary pass so that she could go home for a few hours and finally have her Christmas get-together with her two best friends.

"I can't believe I am finally getting together with them." She was happy to get out of the hospital, if only for a few hours. We stopped at our house to wrap and collect her gifts.

"Winston!" Maddie shouted, as soon as she opened the front door. Winston came flying out, almost knocking her over.

"Careful," I said. "Don't let him jump on you"

"It's okay, he's just excited to see me," she said scratching his ear. His curly tail wagged back and forth. She played with him for a minute, fed him, and dressed him in a funny Hawaiian shirt. Only she could get away with dressing him in such an unbecoming manner. "You look so handsome," she said to Winston, with a twinkle in her eye. He wagged his tail in agreement.

Maddie pulled out her gifts and got down to work. "Mom, I need more wrapping paper," she called out as she prepared to carefully wrap the two presents: perfume for Vicki and a Build-a-Bear for Danielle. I found some in the closet—nothing fancy, it was plain blue—and gave it to her.

"Do you have any Christmas wrap?" she asked.

"Maddie, it's May! You can't get Christmas wrap in May," I exclaimed.

"Okay, fine." She set about wrapping the two gifts. "Do you think they will like them?" she asked nervously.

"Maddie, don't worry, they are perfect, they will love them," I assured her. I dropped her off at Danielle's house. Gifts in hand, she looked excited and happy to see her dear friends and confidants. It really perked her up. "Merry Christmas!" she shouted to me as I drove off.

Two short hours later, I got a call. "Mommy please come and get me, I'm in a lot of pain." Her party was cut short; she was running a fever of 104.

Her friends came out, helping her to the car, carrying her gifts from them. They kept her laughing, distracting her from her obvious pain. Once she was in the car, she gave a weak wave good-bye and I rushed her directly back to the Credit Valley Hospital.

Over the next few days with the fever raging, the staff tried to make Maddie as comfortable as possible. She slept around the clock.

Friday, May 11, the doctors assured me I could leave for a few hours. I went back home to be with Derek. He had won an award of excellence in computers from the school board and was receiving it that morning. I wanted to show my appreciation for all his good work. He, too, had missed out on so much with Maddie being sick. For him to receive this award under such difficult circumstances was amazing. He had been studying on his own, fending for himself, and stressing over his sister. His accomplishment made me extremely proud of him.

Uncle Kevin went to the hospital to stay with Maddie while I was away. I had just arrived back home from Derek's ceremony when I got a call from Kevin. Maddie's condition was worsening; they were transferring her to Sick Kids Hospital immediately. She was on her way by ambulance.

He sounded calm, the words were carefully spoken. I knew he was trying not to alarm me, but I could read between the lines. I panicked. I had to get there quickly, despite the Friday afternoon bumper-to-bumper traffic; I needed my wits about me, or I might get into a car accident. I was terrified that Maddie might die before I got there. As I sat in the slow-moving traffic, helpless, I fought hard to keep calm, praying that Maddie was okay.

She was transferred to the Intensive Care Unit, where she became unresponsive and unable to breathe on her own. With the expertise of about twenty doctors and Maddie's incredible will to beat the cancer, she stabilized by morning. She was put on a ventilator to assist her breathing; received blood and platelet transfusions, and a morphine drip. They hooked up many machines to her, then deeply sedated Maddie to keep her from pulling the tubes out of her mouth.

Maddie was wasting away; the doctors were concerned time was running out. I was terrified. She was in a coma. The doctor said that if she made it through the weekend, they would try to give her the rest of her stem cells (from the transplant the year before), to see if they could help build up her immune system.

I watched her sleep, her bravery beads hanging from her IV pole. I thought how they were not much different than the beads the Maasai warriors in Africa were well-known for wearing; both given for courage. In addition to her school, the drinking well, and her new African friends, they were another connection for her to Africa.

She had hundreds of beads, strings and strings of them in all different colors. Collectively they told the story of her long and difficult journey with cancer. They represented three battles; the third one not yet won. She had been through so much, I prayed for a miracle.

The next night, I tuned the TV in her room to the hockey playoffs. The staff thought I was a little crazy, but it was her beloved Ottawa Senators playing. Maddie had been following them since they first came back as a team in the NHL. I'll never forget how hard it was to get tickets to bring her to a game when she was a young girl. She had been a faithful fan for over a decade. Now, finally, her beloved Ottawa

Senators—with her favorite player and now friend, Wade Redden—were in the playoffs. They were playing the Buffalo Sabres. We loved that team too. If she had been well, there is no doubt we would have been in Buffalo, New York watching the game live.

Even though she was on life support, I was sure she could hear the game. She wasn't able to communicate verbally, but we wanted her surroundings to be as comfortable and as familiar as possible.

I lay on a small cot in her room. The family had gathered out in the visitor's room. No one slept. We waited and prayed.

24

Waiting for Me

*M*ay 13, 2007. "Maddie please, please don't die today," I prayed.

Not today. It was Mother's Day. I couldn't bear it.

I held my daughter ever so gently. I grieved for the beautiful young girl resting lightly in my arms. Her body, ravaged by the reoccurring cancer, weighed barely eighty pounds now. I gently cradled her soft bald head against my wildly beating heart. Her body was warm and still, her breathing labored.

Maddie's beautiful dark hair was all gone, once again, a telling battle sign from a warrior who had fought victoriously twice before. "One more time," I pleaded, "you can do it sweetheart." I held my daughter tightly. I never wanted to let her go. She was my hero.

"I love you baby girl." I told her softly.

I willed her to open her eyes once more. I ached to see those beautiful blue eyes that shone brightly, mirroring her passion for life. Those eyes that first looked lovingly into mine only fifteen short years before, gazing at me with trust. I had never before felt such love; I was full of awe and wonder at that tiny bundle that had instantly stolen my heart.

I remembered being a new mom, terrified of the responsibility of caring for such a small, delicate, precious life that was so vulnerable. We instantly bonded, and I knew we would be okay. I was confident. I would be the best mom ever I had promised her. "I will protect you from harm, and keep you safe," I vowed.

In the Intensive Care Unit, as I held her, I was afraid I had broken that trust and would not be able to save her this time. I grieved for her, for her difficult journey the past three years, the pain, the countless surgeries. I marveled at how heroically she had fought.

I remembered the earlier conversations we had, some really tough topics and discussions for someone so young. I realized, because of her cancer, she had grown up much too quickly. We had talked not only about typical teen challenges, like school, and friends, but the reality of her health and her possible death. I would have done anything to avoid talking about death; she had so much more to live for, to finish. She was a fighter, but she was also wise beyond her years and knew to speak the truth.

I watched a moment longer as she lay resting in my arms, drawing on my inner wisdom, and with a heavy heart, I thought of the unspeakable. My head did not want to acknowledge what my heart knew. Where do we go from here? It felt like we were at a crossroad: a place where life dies, and death lives.

We were Catholics, and Maddie had found solace in attending services at school and at church. She had asked me earlier, "In case they can't control the cancer, would you arrange for me to receive last rites when the time comes." It was important to her, to have this religious rite of passage, her transition from life to death.

I gently rested her head back on her pillow, and with a heavy sigh and a renewed purpose went outside of her room to speak with the hospital's duty social worker. It was Sunday, I arranged for a priest to come in as soon as possible. I feared time was against us. The social worker assured me that he would come the next day.

I couldn't bring myself to go back to Maddie's room just yet. I felt like a failure. My energy was depleted, and I was afraid I would upset her. We were close; at times we could pick up on each other's pain, and emotions. I wanted to spare her from the anguish I was feeling. I went for a lonely walk down the hospital corridor.

As I walked the empty hallways, the only sound was the clicking of my shoes, rhythmic and steady. My feet kept time with the thoughts racing through my mind. I questioned everything I was doing. I had so many doubts. What if we gave her last rites, and she was not dying? Would the ritual scare her, and would she then give up her fight to live? Most of all, I feared that my baby girl was really dying. I tried to banish that thought.

I was so afraid to do the wrong thing that I was paralyzed in my decision-making. I knew the reality of losing a loved one. I thought back to the day my husband died, when I had administered CPR, desperately trying to breathe life back into him. Stephen was a warrior, too. I wasn't able to save him. Is it possible, lightning could strike twice? It wasn't fair.

"Pick me this time," I prayed, "Not my little girl."

How much more could a small body endure? We had put her through hell already; year after year, treatment after treatment, surgery after surgery. We tried every type of chemotherapy that could possibly work. Her body was ravaged, weakened. I couldn't bear the thought that maybe this time her body was beyond repair.

I tried to think straight, block out all the fear, all the guilt, the crazy thoughts. *What should I do?* I asked myself.

"Listen to your heart," I heard a small voice say. I looked around wondering where it was coming from, and saw no one. Was I losing my mind?

"Show me a sign," I responded, unsure and afraid. "Anything."

I needed a sign to show that I was doing the right thing. I paced, I worried and I felt tremendous pain in my heart. I couldn't breathe. I felt defeated; I was losing my faith in science, in God and in myself.

I slowly walked back into her room, and gently held her hand and prayed.

It was a long evening, an endless night full of fear, waves of anxiety, infused with tremendous feelings of pure love for my baby girl. I wanted the world to stop, to freeze in time. I would rather accept being caught in this moment for eternity than the possibility of living in this world without her.

I sat with her, watching her, willing her to open her eyes. She remained quiet and still all night. She was kept barely alive by all the medical equipment. I listened to the rhythm of the machines breathing life into her, buying her time.

I watched her sleep, she looked so beautiful. I remembered how she was always able to light up a room when she entered. Even now with her body ravaged, she still had an effect that touched your soul when you were with her.

The following morning the priest arrived. I tried to calm myself. Was I doing the right thing? He looked nice, priestly looking. I thought, *Now what?*

He introduced himself then he then kindly asked me for my daughter's name.

"Her name is Maddison Babineau," I said.

"Oh," he smiled as he looked at her. He turned his attention back to me. "I have a Babineau in my family, a brother-in-law. Where are you from?"

"Well, my late husband Stephen's family is from the area of Moncton, New Brunswick." I said.

"My brother-in-law is from Moncton too." he replied.

"Really!" That got my attention. I quickly turned to face him. We just looked at each other. I felt a rush of adrenaline wash over me. I knew that a number of Stephen's relatives lived in the Moncton area. My mind was reeling. What did this coincidence mean? Could this priest, who I had never met before, somehow be related to my Maddie and her dad? Even if the connection was only by marriage, what were the odds? Was this the sign I had prayed for?

Did this mean I was doing the right thing? I immediately felt some relief. Was it possible that Stephen was reaching out, letting me know that he was waiting for Maddie, to take care of his firstborn, to reclaim guardianship of his daughter?

Maybe life does goes on. Maybe it's not so much a death, but a transition. I wasn't a believer before, but I've lived an unusual life, full of highs and lows that led me to realize life is full of unexplainable moments. "What is happening here?" I asked my head, my heart, but no clear answer came to me. What if it was true? What if Maddie leaving us now was just a new journey for her?

It felt good to think of the two of them together. Maddie had never seen her father walking. How delighted she would be to have the honor to walk hand-in-hand with her daddy. He had been such a powerful man, full of life before ALS ravaged his body. I began to envision them together, playing and fishing, both their bodies whole, with no disease holding them back. Maddie would finally be pain-free. And, Stephen would be unlocked from the prison that ALS had kept him in.

These happy thoughts allowed me to be distracted from accepting the cold reality that my daughter was gravely ill, receiving her last rites; the sacrament of the sick that prepared for her passage.

The priest gently blessed Maddie while I held her, sending her loving thoughts and prayers. After the last rites were given, I witnessed a single teardrop rolling very slowly down her cheek. Alarmed, I turned to the priest, and blurted out, "Look we've scared her, she's crying. What have we done?"

He looked at me with a wisdom I wasn't tapped into and said, "How do you know it's not tears of joy? You gave her what she asked for, she could be thanking you."

In that moment, I had forgotten that she was incapable of crying. Maddie had been on life support, part of her daily care was receiving drops in her eyes because they kept drying up.

What had we witnessed? Did I imagine it? I looked again and saw the streak of the single tear staining her pale cheek. No, it was real. It was another sign—one I could hardly comprehend at the time. She was letting us know that we did not need to worry any longer, she was okay.

For the rest of the day I did not leave Maddie's side. The last of her harvested stem cells had been administered that morning in the hopes of kick-starting her immune system; a last attempt to save her life. As I sat there, the nurses and doctors worked around the clock to keep her alive. Nothing was working; all of her organs were shutting down. All we could do was wait and pray.

The following day, Tuesday, the doctors told me they were planning on running additional tests to get a better picture of Maddie's condition, and then hold a meeting with the head of the department to discussion the situation.

That afternoon, a specialist put a camera down Maddie's throat to take a better look. Her body barely reacted, no reflexes, no sign of discomfort. I heard one of the doctors say she wasn't responsive. I bit my tongue as I disagreed, I remembered her single tear, I knew she was able to connect when she needed to. Even if they were small, those signs meant everything to me.

A few hours later, they asked me to join the team in the boardroom. It was down the hallway, quite a distance from Maddie's room. I didn't like the idea of being that far away from her, even for a minute. My sister Susan stayed with her as I attended the medical briefing.

I entered the room and saw the team of doctors and social workers in their places around the big table. Each of them had played such a valuable role in my daughter's care. But in the meeting they were focused, matter of fact. I began to feel small and alone, insignificant. I realized nothing was in my control. I was afraid.

The specialist gently explained that they had done all they could to arrest the cancer, but it had continued to spread to Maddie's head and hips. They did not feel any further treatment would be of much benefit. I knew what they were getting at. It was time to accept that Maddie's poor body was ravaged beyond repair. I wanted badly to continue to fight for my daughter, but I knew in my heart she was too frail to win this time.

The idea that Maddie might welcome peace came to me for the first time. After the experience with the priest, a faint thought arose, one that I couldn't have comprehended earlier. Maybe she wanted to go, so maybe now it was okay to let her go. I couldn't believe I was entertaining these thoughts. What kind of mother was I, thinking like this? I loved her; I needed to continue to fight for her, right?

Yet my heart told me the most loving thing to do was to let her go. Free her from her pain. I don't know how I found my voice, but I asked the difficult question, "Might she die in the next day or two?"

At first no one in the room spoke. The question hung in the air. Then softly there was a gentle reply, "Yes." From whom, I wasn't sure.

I asked if I should call all of my family to come in and say a final good-bye.

Again, a "Yes" hung in the air.

Now, I knew the truth. I got up slowly, willing myself to act.

Most of our family had already arrived at the hospital, but there were a few people who needed to be informed of the heartbreaking news. Maddie's grandparents, Derek, aunts and uncles were at the hospital, all taking turns visiting Maddie and praying for her.

Craig Kielburger, co-founder of Free the Children, Maddie's hero, had arrived for a visit and was in her room with her. Her beloved teacher, Mrs. Carducci was also there.

Maddie's best friends were already planning to come in later in the evening from Hamilton. I imagined them getting ready, excited to see her. My best friend, Patti, was on her way from Buffalo. It felt good to know there was so much support at this time.

Shaking, I finally began to accept what I had refused to acknowledge before. With all the courage I had, I said, "Maddie can go now." My heart was breaking as I spoke those words out loud, "Maddie can go and be with her dad."

I took a breath. Silence. No one in the room said a word. Then, the stillness was interrupted by footsteps rushing down the hospital corridor.

"Get Sharon, get Mrs. Babineau. Maddie's is slipping away!" The voice reverberated from the hallway.

I ran back to her room. When I arrived, my sister said the alarms on the machines had started going off.

It appeared that as soon as I said those words out loud—that she could go—the machines that were working so hard moments earlier to keep her alive, couldn't keep up with her failing body.

I wasn't within earshot of her when I said she could go; I was quite far away. How had Maddie heard me?

I didn't understand it at the time, but she had been waiting for me to release her. She was holding on for me. She was waiting until I accepted that it was all right for her to go. She was waiting for me to understand that her life was no longer like ours, that although her body had betrayed her, her spirit would live on. She could go and be in her daddy's arms. She had earned her wings to heaven.

I climbed into bed with her. I could barely get close enough. She had so many cords and wires hooked up to her. The tubes were everywhere, like an octopus with tentacles trying to keep her away from me. I fought for my place as her mother. It was my right, my honor, to hold her as she left this earth, just as I had held her at birth.

I realized it wasn't the machines that had been keeping her alive, it was me. She was willing to endure all the pain until I was able to be at peace with her leaving us. She needed my permission to go, and I had to give it to her. So I lovingly did.

"Good-bye my darling," I said.

Susan brought Derek into the room, and I shared the heartbreaking reality. "Maddie is going to leave us. She is dying," I told him.

They were the most heartbreaking words I had ever uttered. I looked into his eyes and realized that he wasn't expecting her to die. I hadn't prepared him for this moment. She was his big sister, she was his hero. She could do anything. Maddie had always come back from the edge. Now, she was leaving us.

He started crying and begging, "No. No. Maddie don't go. Please don't go."

The two of us held her. The nursing staff quietly turned off the machines. They removed all the tubes and wires so that we could get closer and hold her tight. We held her with all our might. Time stood still.

One of the nurses gently said, "She's gone."

After what seemed like an eternity, Derek slipped out of my arms and quietly left; he was emotionally spent. He was only eleven years old and he had experienced more losses than most people do in a lifetime. He'd lost his father and now his beloved sister.

I continued to lie with Maddie, I held on for dear life until the nurse gently nudged me. She brought me a clean hospital gown, a basin and a clean cloth with which to wash my sweet Maddie.

I slowly got up and stood by the basin. Susan and I very gently began to bathe her. I couldn't take my gaze away from her beautiful face. I gently washed her. Caring for her in this way, it was my last motherly act. I tried desperately to stay in the moment. Not thinking of what I was losing, just touching her, smelling her, taking it all in —capturing this moment, burning it into my memory.

My gaze swept over her body, and how ravished it was. I looked at all the surgical scars; some were recent, still red, some old and faded. They were the marks of a warrior, reflecting all the punishing attempts at trying try to save her.

Her limbs had wasted away. She was light as a feather as we gently turned her over on her stomach so that we could wash her back. As I looked at the long scars on her back, I remembered the jokes she made the day they took the seventy staples out, and I thought of what a fighter she was.

I don't think I loved anyone more than I loved her at that moment. I held her and kissed her, realizing it was for the last time.

Never again was I going to see that smile, or witness her courage, or gain insight from her wisdom. I reflected on how lucky I was that I got to be her mom at all, even if only for fifteen short years. Wonderful memories flooded my senses; all the love, and all of the heartbreak.

I thought of all the times I helped her, picking her up off the bathroom floor day after day, month after month, year after year, frustrated in my inability to take her pain away. I found comfort in the thought that she would no longer have to endure that misery, and I thought of the laughter she shared right up to the end. I knew she had a spirit that couldn't be broken.

In one of the most bizarre moments I could imagine, a nurse came into the room with a food cart, bringing tea, coffee and cookies. I remember looking at her with the snacks and realizing how life just continues.

Then the strangest response came over me. On autopilot, I went to the cart and poured a cup of tea and took a cookie. I sat with the cookie in hand, gazing at my beautiful daughter. I nibbled at it ever so slowly; I was afraid the nurse would come back and take the cart away and make me leave when I was done. I couldn't taste the cookie, but it didn't matter. I didn't believe I would ever be able to desire anything again. Maddie had died. Everything had changed.

I had promised her I would be happy after she was gone. I didn't know how I would be able to keep that promise. Happiness seemed unattainable, ridiculous even.

I understood her powerful message. She loved me and her brother Derek. I knew that she wanted to make sure that he would always be loved and he deserved living in a happy home. She was always looking out for her little brother. Somehow, I knew we would get through this together.

I silently prayed: *Give me the strength to have half the courage my daughter had.*

I kissed her for the final time. Always considered a precious gift from God, I would never forget this day: May 15, 2007, the day I gave my gift back.

As I quietly closed the door to her room, I sensed she wasn't gone from us. We had gained an angel to watch over us.

25

Snow White Sleeps

Walking down the hospital corridor I leaned against my mom for comfort, my head resting on her shoulder, both of us struggling to hold ourselves together. Nothing could alleviate our pain.

Leaving the hospital without my sweet Maddie was the hardest thing I had ever done. Losing a husband was difficult enough, but this was unthinkable. I was emotionally exhausted, my heart was numb.

Surrounded by family, we went quietly down the Sick Kids Hospital elevator for the last time, into the underground garage. Weak with grief, I was helped into the back of the vehicle, where my family formed a loving circle around me. Normally I would be in the driver's seat, taking a back seat was symbolic; I was no longer in control.

My face pressed against the cool window of the van, I willed all of this to be a bad dream. The thought of going back to "our" home where my daughter's bed would be forever empty, was unbearable. My hands reached out to hold Maddie's one more time, but she wasn't there to receive them. I placed them on my lap instead, an empty, despondent gesture.

At home I couldn't sleep. In my head I began to plan my beautiful daughter's funeral. I took comfort in knowing that family and friends would rally to ensure that everything that needed to be done would be done. Yet, no matter how much help those around me provided, I knew I had to make many difficult decisions that no parent ever wants to make.

It was a heartbreaking task; yet, I instinctively knew her funeral needed to have a different tone, something as uplifting as she had been. I wondered how I could make it a safe place for those attending; not too dreary or depressing. It had to be more of a celebration of Maddie, of the wonderful young woman she had become under the most difficult of circumstances. She needed to be remembered for her caring nature and all the good that she had done while she was alive.

I wanted the service to be a remarkable experience and a safe place for her young friends to grieve. If I was overwhelmed, I could just imagine how Maddie's friends were feeling. They were at an age of vulnerability and for many of them this was their first experience with death.

As I lined up the list of tasks to accomplish, the first one was the most difficult: choosing of her coffin. My brother drove me to the funeral home to discuss the arrangements. The funeral director brought us into a room lined with coffins. As I walked past them, I asked, "Could there be one that is not so . . . um . . . intimidating?" What I meant was, one that did not really look like a coffin.

Yes, there was one that was different. It was porcelain white and was constructed in a shiny material that was made in a way so that people could write their farewells on it. With this coffin, I was able to design the inside backsplash. I selected a beautiful mural—it was an African scene, bright orange sunset with an African silhouette of elephants and zebras feeding in the distance. On the right side was Maddie's smiling face with the caption, "The girl who gave her wish away." In the picture, she looked alive and vibrant.

I purchased different colored markers for the guests to use to write their personal messages to Maddie. I felt the idea of leaving a message on Maddie's casket might make it easier for them to say good-bye. Perhaps this was the best way for everyone to find closure after all the years of cheering her on. This would be a gesture of peace. I didn't want them to be afraid of getting too close to her.

Derek and I wanted to do one last special act for Maddie. Prior to the funeral, we went to the Build-a-Bear store at the mall to get a new stuffed animal to put in her coffin. Derek could not part with Maddie's old one.

We duplicated the one she loved so much: a Hello Kitty stuffed animal with a Spiderman costume. Together, with tears in our eyes, we taped a heartfelt message for her, "We love you Maddie, you will never be forgotten" and we sealed it with a kiss. The heart with the message was placed inside the animal's chest and we carefully stitched it up.

When we arrived at the funeral home for the first viewing, I approached the coffin with Derek by my side. I had to brace myself to look inside. There she was, lying so peacefully before me, looking just like Snow White. She had on her wig, her pink headband and her grade eight graduation dress. Her skin was as white as the porcelain coffin. She was beautiful. She looked like she was in a peaceful sleep.

I kissed her. Like the prince in the story, I wished I had the power to wake her up—but that was a fairy tale and this was real life.

Derek lovingly placed the stuffed animal beside her in the coffin.

The public viewing started at 7:00 P.M. and we were overwhelmed by the number of friends and family who arrived to say their last good-byes. They were strongly united in their grief. It became more and more obvious that they, too, had lost someone who meant more to them than I could have imagined. Many people left gifts and trinkets as a sign of their love and desire to somehow leave a part of themselves with her.

For two days, a steady line of guests arrived for the viewing. By the second day, the coffin no longer displayed its original shiny white cover. It was covered with messages and images of heartfelt love, from the emblem of the Ottawa Senators to drawings of angels, and many sincere good-byes. It was now a loving piece of art, a mosaic of colors.

My heart swelled with pride as I heard the many stories from people of all ages. One elderly man shared that he carried Maddie's picture around in his wallet, and a woman who was a stranger shared that she kept a picture of Maddie in her Bible.

The messages included:

"We need more people like her in the world."

"I love you and I don't even know you. All I know is that you are amazing."

"You showed us how we all have it in us to change the world."

"After a moment's exchange with her, one developed a desire to change the world as well."

A message left on Maddie's web page said it all:

"Maddie—you are pain free at last.

Now it is our turn to feel the pain of losing you."

A young girl called me the day after Maddie passed away. She had left a voicemail message, and she sounded a bit nervous. She had known and admired Maddie. She asked if she could sing at the funeral. She said she would be honored to have the opportunity. She elaborated breathlessly, not to worry, that she had a beautiful voice and that she had won awards in the past.

It was one of those moments when you just trust the unusual turn of events. I simply had to believe it would be perfect. I called the number she had left and her mother answered. She was excited when I told her that we would be honored to have her daughter sing at Maddie's funeral. I requested she sing Josh Groban's "You Raise Me Up." I didn't realize it at the time, but she had never performed that song in public. She quickly practiced and perfected the song.

The day of Maddie's funeral was a sunny one. As we pulled up in the funeral procession, the church was already packed with over 400 mourners.

I held on to Derek tightly, and watched my brothers, stepfather and nephews carry Maddie's coffin into the church. We were met by a long line of Maddie's friends standing at attention—a special honor guard for Maddie. Their forlorn expressions said it all. We were all heartbroken.

Maddie's Aunt Sue, Stephen's younger sister, and cousins arrived from Ottawa. Sue adored Stephen and spent as much time as she could with him when we were in Ottawa. Cousin David commented that he was amazed as he walked through town. On every corner newspaper stand, he could see Maddie's beautiful face gracing the front page of the *Hamilton Spectator*. It was clear her community loved her.

As we entered the church with Maddie's coffin, everyone listened for the sound of the church bell, the traditional announcement of the arrival of the deceased. A bell wasn't needed to let us know Maddie was there because she gave us her own signs! At the exact moment she arrived, the candle at the altar went out on its own and a glass at the front of the church fell, and shattered on the floor. The noise startled everyone. She was telling me again that she was with me, reminding me she was okay.

I had lovingly chosen the readings for the service. The funeral mass was ninety minutes long. Deep in my grief, I had trouble focusing. I clutched my tissue in one hand, and held onto Derek with the other.

Derek had offered to read a passage. I watched as he slowly walked to the front of the church and stood at the podium. He held his head high and started to read. He had a beautiful voice, sincere and passionate. Though hurting, he somehow got through it. He wasn't going to show his sadness; he was strong for his big sister.

We celebrated her life.

When the Mass was over, the girl went up to perform the Josh Groban song. She sang beautifully and with so much emotion that there wasn't a dry eye in the church.

After the service, we left in a long funeral procession to the cemetery. My family travelled with me; we sat lost in our own thoughts, barely saying a word. I closed my eyes; I needed to compose myself for this next difficult task.

Hundreds of people greeted us at the gravesite to say their final good-byes. Maddie's coffin stood out, with its colorful drawings and loving farewells painted all over it. A representation of her vibrant life, it was a stark contrast to the dull tombstones. We gathered around it in a large circle.

With a mixture of tears and joyful remembrance, we said our final good-byes and placed flowers on her coffin. Our last loving gesture was the release of a hundred colored balloons. We stood there bathed in the sunshine for a long time, mesmerized by their purposeful flight, up, up, till they were out of sight.

That afternoon we held a special luncheon at Michelangelo's Banquet Center, where we celebrated her life. People made toasts to Maddie: a young girl who, although incredibly shy, found her voice by speaking up for others. She had made a difference and in turn every person there felt that they, too, had the ability to make one. People gave speeches and told funny stories—about fingers stuck in garage doors, frozen peas, and trips to the beach. It was a time to rejoice in the beautiful person that was my daughter.

When I returned home, I was so emotionally spent I could barely open the front door. Hands weak, I dropped my keys, and as I straightened up, I noticed a letter in the mailbox. I brought it in with me. It was addressed to Maddie. My heart skipped a beat. Should I open it? I hesitated, took a breath, then I slowly tore it open. The postage showed it had been mailed just before Maddie died.

I pulled out the letter, and I noticed it had been written by a child. The young girl had decided to skip getting birthday presents that year and instead asked for people to give her the money that they would have spent on her gifts so that she could donate it to Maddie's project with Free the Children. There was $320.00 in the envelope.

I held the letter tightly in my hands, the words blurring because of my tears. Catching bits and pieces, it read: "Dear Maddie . . . you're amazing . . . I want to make a difference too . . ." I breathed in the meaning of the words and actions, realizing Maddie *did* have a legacy.

In that moment, I felt Maddie with me. She would never really be gone or forgotten.

I smiled at the thought of her impacting lives long after her death. "One bright life, like one drop of water in the ocean; how far reaching would her ripple effect be?"

Maddie taught me an extraordinary life lesson, and it is one that now guides the way I live my life. When I want to hide from the world, because the pain from my aching heart is so raw I can barely breathe, I turn inward and seek out her beautiful spirit. She gave me purpose with my promise to her. "Be happy after I'm gone," she had pleaded. These words that once haunted me are now my source of inspiration.

At first, it was difficult to imagine that happiness could ever be in the cards for me. But I needed to honor Maddie's courage, Stephen's courage, and their unwavering spirits. Most importantly, I needed to live a full life to honor their memory.

I put on a brave face as I went about my daily routine. To the rest of the world, my life appeared normal, but on the inside I was shattered and fragile. I asked myself endless questions about what I could or should have done things differently. I blamed myself for not knowing that she had cancer earlier, for not fighting harder, and I blamed myself for not finding a cure.

Adding to my heartache, I had received an unexpected call from my supervisor. I had taken a leave of absence from work on medical (stress) leave during Maddie's relapse. I had planned to return and looked forward to digging in and making a difference again. However, just before Maddie passed away, I was told that my job was no longer available. They were hiring someone to take it over. I was devastated by this unexpected turn of events; I had worked and volunteered for them for many years, winning awards, putting my heart and soul into my job. Now it, too, was gone. I didn't think I could handle any more bad news. With no job awaiting me, we would be facing further financial problems. I was at my breaking point. With too much free time on my hands it was becoming very easy to engage in self-pity.

Derek was my lifeline; he made me laugh when I wanted to cry, and he gave me hope when I wanted to give up, and he loved me unconditionally. He gave me a reason to get up every day.

I made many visits to Maddie's grave, tending to the flowers and reading the heartfelt notes that her friends left during their frequent visits. I would sit silently with my grief. One day, after placing a single red daisy on her gravestone, I got down on my knees and poured out my heart to her.

"Maddie, it isn't fair. You made me promise I would be happy. I want to be happier for Derek's sake, I do. But you didn't tell me how!"

I pleaded, "I need to know how. How can I be expected to be happy when life is so cruel?" I begged for an answer. "Can I take it back . . . the promise . . . please?"

I knew in my heart the answer was "NO."

It was all up to me. I had to figure it out myself. This was my journey, just like she had her journey. How was it she was so strong and wise at such a young age? What could I learn from her? I had watched as she blossomed into a beautiful young woman, and how she took the focus off of her cancer and onto her cause, the young children in Africa. This is what made her happy.

I was so wrapped up in my grief; I hadn't realized where my focus had been—on poor old me. Maybe that was why I felt so sick, withdrawn, and anxious. Of course, I was mourning, but maybe others were hurting and needed my help. I tried to feel more positive about moving forward and helping others.

Something shifted in my awareness, leaving me feeling more connected to others. It wasn't a big "AHA" moment, but a dawning, a powerful realization that opened up like a beautiful unexpected gift: people cared. Everywhere I went the first few months after Maddie's death, people—strangers—went out of their way to tell me how special Maddie was to them, how her courage inspired them. Strangers who recognized me from TV or my picture in the newspaper, stopped to embrace me in restaurants, grocery stores, and even public washrooms.

The hole in my heart began to heal by the serendipitous moments of caring and kindness from strangers, family and friends. They would tell me I was a great mom, that I should be so proud. They would take money out of their wallets and donate to Maddie's cause right on the spot, no matter where we were. These were the moments that helped me through my grieving and gradually I no longer felt alone.

It was a very gradual process and each day presented its own challenges. Holidays seemed to be the worst. The first Thanksgiving without Maddie everything went wrong. The turkey was undercooked, dinner was late, and I was in a very bad mood. Maddie had always helped me with the preparations and it just seemed unbearable without her.

I'd had enough. I threw the raw turkey back into the oven, slammed the door and broke down crying. I sobbed, "I can't do this, I just can't. I'm not strong enough." I kept saying it over and over again. I felt discouraged and defeated.

While I was having this meltdown, a part of me was chastising, "Hold it together. You've been through worse. You're a decorated military soldier. You've driven tanks, thrown grenades, been gassed, climbed the highest freestanding mountain in the world. You cared for your husband, and your daughter died in your arms! Now you are crying over an uncooked turkey! Seriously, shame on you."

The tough talk wasn't working, this was different. My mind said, "I'm not a tough soldier now; I'm a grieving mom who has lost her child. It's a game-changer." I felt so lost.

As I sat on the kitchen floor crying, I heard a familiar sound— *blip blip, blip, blip*—my computer was alerting me to a newly arrived email message. I wiped my tears on the sleeve of my favorite blue shirt and went to see who the email was from. I welcomed any distraction, even junk mail.

The message read: "Dear Mrs. Babineau, you don't know me. I hope I am not bothering you. I just read Maddie's story and I wanted to tell you that she was amazing, and I think that you are the strongest person I have ever known."

I looked at the computer screen, wondering if this was some kind of a cosmic joke. Was I hallucinating? My eyes burned from the tears as I reread it. "You are the strongest person I have ever known."

I was thrilled that the young boy who wrote the email had been inspired by Maddie, but how did he know to say these words to me at this exact moment when I was overwhelmed and truly in need of positive encouragement? They were the same words I had just used, but I used them in a powerless and negative way. No, of course, he wasn't bothering me, I wanted to shout; just the opposite. I had goose bumps as I again experienced another moment of connectedness to the universe. I knew without any doubt that I was not alone.

Somehow I would get through this, remembering that I had made a promise that I fully intended to keep.

Derek continued to be the most amazing son, never complaining as he became my constant companion and supporter. He would not leave my side, nor would he play outdoors with his friends unless he knew I was okay. I realized he needed me to be okay in order for him to be okay. I had to lead by example. I had to be brave for his sake.

I had some serious soul-searching to do. I thought about Maddie and how she never really complained. She had so many choices to make during her illness. She could have responded in many ways: by rightfully being angry, hurt and sad; or being accepting, courageous and happy. She chose to be grateful to her friends and family, and the people who supported her, and was happy in her efforts to help others.

What made her most happy was having a purpose, something bigger than herself. Even in her weakest state, she cared about the lives of the children in Africa. She actually lived life fully with a powerful vision.

I saw her grateful under the most trying of circumstances. When her hair first fell out, she was grateful the chemotherapy was working. When she received her wish, she gratefully gave it away. When she knew she was dying, instead of being angry or afraid, she reached out to us to help her make a difference in the world. Her wish was now multiplying by the efforts being done in her memory.

Author Robert Holden said, "The miracle of gratitude is that it shifts your perception to such an extent that it changes the world you see." I needed to change my perspective, to see life differently. I had chosen sadness, anger and suffering. I knew deep down, I had much to be grateful for. I had to rethink what was really important in my life and how I wanted to live it.

Maddie had energized me with her unwavering spirit, realizing her life purpose, and moving courageously forward even during her illness. She did what she needed to do with passion and purpose. She understood what it meant to live without self-pity, giving to the children in another part of the world, who she believed suffered far greater than she did. She shared her lessons in the most constructive way, by being the example that taught us humility.

I wanted to keep Maddie's dream alive. I trusted that all the wonderful supporters, friends, even strangers that had helped me heal, would help me continue her dream—her legacy.

I finally understood the secret to being happy. It comes from taking the focus off of ourselves, even in our most difficult times. I would channel my grief with a positive effort, making a difference by reaching out and helping others, like Maddie did. This would bring happiness, giving me hope and purpose.

Epilogue

An Everlasting Wish

August 2007, Hijacked to Africa

*G*etting hijacked sounds like something that only happens in action-adventure movies or some awful criminal activity. It's certainly not something any sane person would look forward to but, when it happened to me, I was thrilled.

The adventure happened at a time in my life when I needed a lifeline, something to care about. This opportunity provided exactly that.

Months earlier, while in the hospital with Maddie, I had come across an ad about a new show coming to Canadian television called *No Opportunity Wasted*, inspired by the life philosophy of Phil Keoghan, host of the popular reality series *The Amazing Race*.

The Amazing Race was one of Maddie's favorite shows. Watching it together in the hospital, we had travelled the world without ever leaving her hospital room; the program was a wonderful break from the monotonous hours spent in bed recovering from one treatment, and waiting for the next.

The ad called for applications for the new series. I was intrigued by the special episode called *Aim for the Heart*. The producers were looking for two people to participate in a travel challenge that brought help to others. I wistfully thought it would be a perfect adventure for Maddie and me to take. If I applied for her, I hoped that when the producers heard about Maddie and how she gave her wish away they would be inspired enough to choose us for this segment. That they would take us to Africa so Maddie could personally see her school and the well she had built with so much of her heart.

Coincidentally, they were holding an audition right near the hospital the same week Maddie would be in Toronto. I thought maybe I could go to the audition on her behalf. But Maddie wasn't well that day, and I certainly wasn't going to leave her side for a pipedream.

After Maddie passed away, I put the thought of auditioning and going to Africa out of my mind. I couldn't imagine going without her.

In July, I was encouraged by my family and Craig Kielburger to reconsider and apply to the show, to go in Maddie's place. At the time, I had no idea that the producer, Morgan Elliott, had already learned of Maddie's story from the local paper and was interested in taking me. All I needed to do was apply. I did.

If you were picked, they would "hijack", or surprise you. With the help of the participant's family, the TV crew would show up unexpectedly and take the challenger away on an adventure of a lifetime.

In late August, a week after I had even stopped thinking about the possibility of being chosen, Bruce Kirkby, host of the show, appeared at my doorstep with a camera crew in tow and swept me away for this amazing expedition. My bags had been packed for me; we left right then and there.

Derek and Kevin joined me on the trip. We flew to Nairobi, then on to the Maasia Mara, where the Free the Children compound was located. We landed in a barren field—nothing in sight except a few zebras. Then, out of the brush, a crowd of children came rushing toward us, all smiles and eager to greet us. We couldn't understand their language, but there was no barrier. They wanted high-fives and greeted us with the saying we would soon be very familiar with, *"Jambo!"*

A young girl slipped her warm little hand in mine and looked up at me with complete trust. I was immediately connected with her beautiful smiling face. It was just like we saw on TV. It was the first of what would be many occasions that I was truly touched by African generosity, love for life, and spirit. These were the children that had touched my daughter's heart. I was in Africa. I had to pinch myself.

We followed a dirt path to the Free the Children compound. It was about an hour-long walk. We just enjoyed the moment, with goats and kids following us. Some walked behind us, some beside us.

The children's clothes were mismatched; most of them walked without shoes. Laughing and singing, the kids herded the goats, whose bells chimed in rhythm as we walked. I was touched by how excited and happy they were to see us.

There were a couple of Maasai warriors, in their bright red custom dress and decorative beading, waiting to escort us into the compound. The weather was beautiful, not too hot. Our escorts' names were Wilson and Willie.

They took us to Free the Children's Kenya School of the Savannah Leadership Center, a beautiful place. We were introduced to the mostly African staff.

Tara Stewart, the other challenger who was a teacher from Prince Edward Island, and I were officially introduced to each other on camera and had our first interview with Bruce Kirkby. He noted that for the seventy-two hours we were there, we were not just visitors, but were there to really experience life in Africa. We were going to immerse ourselves in the life of the Maasai region, help to dig Maddie's well, haul water, and cook a meal. We were energized and ready to accept all challenges.

We were warned to get a good night's sleep as there was lots for us to do during the three-day challenge. We headed back to the compound where we were given a wonderful dinner, and were introduced to Chai tea. The meal was typical Canadian fare with lots of local spices; a nice combination. We ate, and then sat by a big fireplace. It was soon dark, and when the generator for electricity was turned off at 8:00 P.M. we were in total darkness. A stone path lit by lanterns guided us to our sleeping quarters. Armed Maasai warriors escorted us to our residences. Their weapons were to protect us from any wildlife that might get into the compound.

A fire was set when we got back to our rooms. Derek, Kevin and I had a beautiful stone house to stay in. Mosquito-netting covered the beds to protect us from the biting insects — and malaria. The place was absolutely breathtakingly peaceful.

I was too excited to sleep. I wanted to absorb the magic of actually being in Africa. I was kept awake by unfamiliar noises in the air: bush monkeys, birds, and other creatures of the night.

I awoke feeling like I was still in a dream, breathing in the distinct African air and the strange sounds outside. I quickly got up, eager to start my day. There was a shower in the bathroom. I jumped in but the cold, brown water quickly reminded that this was not North America. I realized it was a real feat to have running water, and a flush toilet, in this rural community.

We had breakfast and headed out to Maddie's school to start our first task.

Bruce Kirkby introduced us to the local elders. The women were very friendly. I couldn't tell how old they were. Physically, they looked weathered by the elements and the difficult lives they led, but they had a powerful presence and much wisdom.

I wanted to share Maddie's story; I had to be careful of the meaning. It was Maddie's message of caring for the children of Africa that was much more important than the fact that I had lost a child to cancer. Here, one in five children do not survive to age five, many have lost their parents, and have no access to education or food.

I didn't want the sadness of losing Maddie to be the focus, and overshadow the wonderful work she and her friends and community had done. The message I wanted to deliver to the children of Africa was that people halfway around the world cared about them and wanted to help.

I shared Maddie's story with some of the women elders who gathered to meet us. They listened intently and with compassion. They were touched by Maddie's story. They felt empathy towards me as a mother, and opened up and shared some of their own heartbreaking stories. Many had lost children. Some were caring for their grandchildren or other children who were orphaned by the AIDS crisis. I was in awe of their strength and courage.

I couldn't wait to visit the school: the Motony Primary School in the Oloomirani region. Each one-room building contained a single classroom and there was one grade per building. Maddie's school housed the seventh grade class. I imagined her in this room. The children were the same age Maddie had been when she was diagnosed with cancer.

There were to be eight school rooms built in that compound. Across from Maddie's, a new building had just been completed the weekend before we arrived.

We walked over to the little classroom that Maddie's wish had provided. It was bare. There was a row of windows, twenty small wooden desks, and a chalkboard centered on the front wall. Nothing else adorned the walls.

It was a stark contrast to the abundance in our schools back home; no computers, no books, no visual aids, no libraries, no playground. Each student had just a small workbook and a few pencils. The children here were clearly grateful for this place, and the opportunity to get an education. I was surprised to learn that they were not only taught in Swahili, but they were also learning English.

We danced and sang, and connected through our stories. We created memories I will never forget.

All of the young kids had shaved heads; they were fascinated by Derek's long hair. They would sneak up on him, knock his baseball cap off his head and giggle at him. One brave young girl came up to him and touched and played with his hair. By the end of the trip, he was so relaxed he would allow them to braid his hair for fun.

Food was scarce, so when it was time for us and the crew to break from filming to eat, we had to go sit in our vehicles or drive a distance away—have our picnic out of sight. It was difficult to know that these sweet children were going hungry while we were being fed so well. While I wanted to share, I knew offering one sandwich wasn't the solution. Free the Children was working hard to solve the hunger problem and succeeding with gardens near the school.

The next day, we got to meet Masharia, the foreman in charge of digging Maddie's well. It became a community event; everyone came to help out. We spent the day digging out the reservoir. We worked till we had blisters. The only tools we had were small shovels. Again, I thought of home, and how privileged we were. This job with the right equipment could be done in a few hours. However, without the proper tools, the work was slow, arduous and backbreaking.

I didn't dare complain. I knew how lucky we were, how we lived a privileged life. We turn on a tap and the hot and cold water simply appears. We don't have to think about it, and because it is so easy, sometimes we are not grateful for it.

The following day, our task was to set out to do everything needed to complete a typical African village meal. First, we had to cut wood and haul it back. They gave me a machete to use to cut the kindling. We were sent down the road to collect the brush. We had to use the machete to break the branches. The villagers gathered and watched us. I struggled under the weight of the machete.

The villagers watched intently, finally they couldn't bear it anymore. They laughed at how badly I handled it. I was awkward and unsure and clearly very funny to watch in action. When they went to work, they were at ease; they carried their children on their backs into the fields. Tara was trusted with carrying a young baby while also carefully balancing a stack of wood on her back. As we walked back, they broke into song. We learned they were always breaking out in song, full of life.

Next, we fetched water for the meal. We followed a path for miles to get to the nearest river. At one point in the narrow path, we encountered an area where an electric fence guarded one side, and brushes with thorns aligned the other side. The fence lined the property of a rich landowner. We could barely squeeze by. As I passed by, I worried how the mamas did this difficult trip with small children on their backs.

After forty-five minutes, we arrived at the river—the main water supply. I looked around noting that not only was it a place where they washed their clothes, they also tethered animals there. It was their only source of drinking water and this water was definitely not safe to drink or cook with. The problem was that with no sanitation or bathrooms, many of the villagers relieved themselves in the fields; that waste flowed into the same river where they got their water. Unfortunately, preventable waterborne diseases took many lives.

We were given large water jugs to fill and carry back. One of the women helped me get ready for the task. She showed me how to use the straps around my head to support the jug. I was intimidated when I picked it up. It was so heavy; it immediately caused severe pain in my neck and shoulders. Tara's task was even more difficult, she was given a larger water jug than I had. We looked at each other, not sure we could accomplish the job at hand.

As I struggled with the heavy jug on the long walk back, I realized, Maddie's well would not only provide safe drinking water, it would save the women and children from enduring the long daily trip—a double blessing.

We ground the corn that would be the simple meal of corn mush. It took us hours to prepare. After boiling the water and simmering the mush, called *ugali*, we brought it out to serve to all the kids and mamas who had gathered to see us. I was honored to serve them this simple meal.

From one large bowl, I was told to give each person a spoonful of *ugali*. One by one, they gratefully took the spoonful of food and put it in their mouths. That was all. That was their meal. No milk. No juice. No bread. No fruit. No meat. No vegetable.

I thought of how we ate back home, our abundance of food. And, I thought of the waste, and the thrown-out leftovers. I felt ashamed; I knew I had to make changes in my life once I got back home. No matter who you are, this place opens your eyes, awakens your consciousness, and softens your heart.

The seventy-two hour challenge was quickly coming to an end, though I didn't want it to. The trip had been timed so that our last day coincided with the children's first day of school. I jumped out of bed excited by my expectations of what the day would bring. I walked around the cottage for the last time, taking it all in. I greeted Derek and Kevin as they came out of their room.

"Well this is it," I said sadly.

"Mom, I had an amazing time. I'm so glad we had the chance to do this together," Derek said. He gave me a big hug, knowing I was thinking about Maddie. He still watched out for me.

We drove out in the Jeep with the camera crew to capture the first day of school. I was surprised and thrilled to see that there were hundreds of children, all benefiting from these small schoolhouses. It seemed like such a large number. When we looked out over the horizon, there were only a scattering of mud huts. Where did they all come from?

These children must have walked for miles to come to school. For them it was a pleasure, a highly regarded privilege not to be wasted. The teachers also came from far away, dedicated to supporting the youth in their community.

The children danced and sang for us, and we even learned a few Swahili songs to join in with them. We were honored with a special celebration and dedication in Maddie's honor. They presented a plaque to me that today hangs on the drinking well in remembrance of Maddie. We exchanged M.A.D. 4 MADDIE (Making a Difference for Maddie) bracelets with the mamas, and in return received handmade necklaces.

As we prepared to leave, I knew this was an experience I would never forget. My eyes were opened; my heart touched, and my life was changed. This was a special place where I felt close to Maddie. Her spirit, her legacy, would always be carried on through the school, the well, and these precious children.

March 2012

Once back from Africa, Derek and I were determined that Maddie's dream would live on. We were so grateful for our experience there. It inspired us to embrace life fully, with no opportunity wasted, and to live as compassionately as Maddie did.

The memories of the children we met would be our driving force. Maddie's passion for life was the spark that ignited our passion. With her death, she had passed the torch to all of us: birthing her legacy, *Maddie's Everlasting Wish,* a not-for-profit organization founded in her memory. She lives on through the good work that continues.

I am very grateful to the wonderful youth who work so hard keeping Maddie's legacy alive. It is their passion now. They know that they, too, can change the world and they are doing it. Over the next five years, along with a group of dedicated volunteers, we passionately raised funds through annual 5K runs, dinners, dances and silent auctions.

Through M.A.D. 4 MADDIE, we raised funds for the Baraka Health Clinic in Kenya and for building a maternity ward.

On the fifth anniversary of Maddie's death, Derek and I made the trip back to Africa. After flying to Nairobi, we went to the small airport where we would board the small Cessna that would take us back to Maasia Mara.

As we approached the small plane, I stretched to see who would be piloting it. As I got closer I saw that the pilot was a female. I couldn't believe it. I smiled as I rushed over to greet her. "May I take a picture with you, please?" I gushed.

"Sure, she replied, humoring 'the tourist'." Her name was Sadiki.

I got close to her and hoped and prayed that my camera was charged. "Derek!" I shouted. "Please come quickly and take our picture." I was as excited as I would to meet a favorite movie star. I'm sure I embarrassed Derek but I could not help myself. She was beautiful, vibrant and confident. She represented the potential of all the young girls in Africa; all they needed was access to an education.

This reinforced my belief in the importance of having schools. Now I had experienced the pleasure of witnessing it!

We flew out of the city, and watched as the scenery changed to barren lands with few buildings. There were mostly huts made of grass, stick, mud and cow dung. I knew we were getting close. We landed at a small airstrip. Our pilot helped us exit the plane, then erased our footsteps with a broom, sweeping the dirt to smooth out the runway, which really was just a dirt path.

I looked at Derek. The last time we'd been here, he was a small boy with long hair. This time he was almost six feet tall, a young man with short hair, and a mature attitude, sharp-witted, confident, and easygoing. Everyone commented on his pleasant demeanor: always smiling, a pleasure to be around. His sister would have been proud.

We were greeted by the staff from Free the Children, and were delighted to see them all again. High-fives and lots of hugs and hand-shaking were the normal greetings.

The next week was filled with a whirlwind of activities. We visited Maddie's school; it was summertime, so school was out, but young local kids came running out to greet us and play with us. There were about eight young boys from the ages of four to maybe twelve. It was hard to accurately guess their ages; they were much smaller than the kids back home due to malnutrition.

Their clothes were dirty and tattered, but what stood out most were their eyes and their smiles. They genuinely seemed so happy, so curious. I couldn't help but feel connected and smiled back.

A young girl, about six years old, effortlessly balancing a small baby on her back, ran and played, easily keeping up with us. The baby boy peeked out at us. I couldn't believe someone so young was entrusted with the daily care of a baby. It seemed the young girls never had any real free time. That is a fact of life here, I reminded myself; that is why we were so committed to helping them.

We visited the Baraka Health Clinic. This much-needed new facility offers curative and preventative services to everyone on an outpatient basis. Incredibly, they serve over 40,000 people in the community.

I wondered where they came from. The countryside is so barren; there is no industry, no large buildings, no commerce. They must have to walk for many miles to get there.

The clinic was much bigger than I had imagined. I was in awe of the amount of energy and commitment that went into the planning and design. There were labs, gardens, ambulance service, pharmaceuticals, supplements, treatment rooms, and many more services.

We met the staff and heard about all the good work they were doing there. Lives were being saved, children were healthier, there was less preventable illnesses in the community; all wonderful news.

We visited the Kisaruni Girls Secondary School. They had been waiting patiently for us. We arrived to a brilliant dance performance. They playfully brought us on stage to join them. They laughed good-naturedly as we floundered and misstepped awkwardly through the simple dance routine. Not knowing Swahili makes the straightforward "step left," "step right" instruction difficult to grasp. We were their guests for the rest of the afternoon.

They served us tea, and cookies. I sat with a group of young girls around Maddie's age — 15 to 16. They told me their dreams. I learned quickly that they dream big: Mercy wanted to be an engineer; Sharon a doctor (she laughed when she learned we have the same first name); Mary a lawyer. They were articulate, bright-eyed and eager to do well. I felt their sense of desire to serve their community, to give back. I had no doubt they would attain their dreams.

I shared Maddie's story. Some of them already knew of her. Mercy actually attended Maddie's school and had knowledge of her life story. I got goose bumps when she shared this connection with me. They presented me with a hand drawn thank-you card, as a token of their appreciation.

They changed into bright orange-and-red sports uniforms, and challenged us to a game of soccer and basketball. We spent a playful afternoon outdoors. The landscape, the mountains, unusual-looking trees and wandering animals in the background seemed surreal. I took it all in. A whistle blew, and sadly, we had to leave; they had chores and homework to do. I wished them all the best and imagined every one of them using this education to live extraordinary lives.

The highlight of the trip was working on the maternity ward. The building design was much more elaborate than I had anticipated. The outer walls were almost up, so walking through the interior we had to imagine what it would eventually look like. As we went through each "room," I envisioned a young mother arriving in labor and having a safe, sterile birthing room—just like I did when I gave birth to my two children. Then there was a room for her to rest overnight, to keep both mom and baby safe.

The center would also provide prenatal help during pregnancy, increasing the women's chances of having safe births, strong babies, and healthy recoveries. I remembered how scared I had been the first time I gave birth and all the support that was available to me. I was excited for all the mothers who would enter this wonderful facility. Maddie had always wanted to be a mom. I think of Maddie as their guardian.

We were invited to help work on building the outer walls. For three glorious days we were busy, mixing cement, plastering, and getting down and dirty. Every day started with getting up early, taking the long trip from the Free the Children compound down the bumpy, potholed, dusty road in a big, bus-sized, off-road vehicle, and then working for hours in the heat. I felt really connected and blessed to be there working on such a significant project.

On the last day of working on the wall I thought about the purple bracelet I was wearing. It was soft plastic and had M.A.D. 4 MAD-DIE stamped on it. We had a thousand of them made, and sold them for $3 each to help raise money for the clinic and maternity ward. I impulsively took the one I was wearing off my wrist and slipped it into a crack and caringly cemented it into the wall, wanting to leave a bit of Maddie behind for good luck for all who entered.

As I stepped on the bus, I was bursting with pride for all the work Maddie did and all the amazing work that was continuing to be done by the countless dedicated people over the past five years. Maddie's life purpose had indeed become our purpose: to change the world, to make a difference. I smiled as I reflected on the truth in what Maddie had taught me: we find happiness by reaching out and helping others.

That is the Magic of Maddie, and that is the magic that is in all of us. If anyone tells you that you can't make a difference, or can't change the world, don't believe it. Maddie did it, and we all can too.

I didn't want to leave this beautiful country, a place where they may not have ample opportunity and material possessions, but their love for life, their endearing optimism, more than makes up for it. It made me think we might have it backwards. Maybe we are the ones lacking; with too much stuff and not enough community, connection, and kindness.

I knew I would have difficulty adjusting on my return to the crazy commercialized world we live in. I envisioned my life changing, becoming freer, less attachment to things, and more openness to helping others.

I turned back for one last look at the Baraka Health Clinic and Maternity Ward. My heart skipped a beat; the road I was on looked very familiar. I realized it looked just like the road in the TV show that Maddie had been watching when she first saw the faces of the African children. It was where that young boy once walked so alone and afraid; the road that opened up Maddie's world and her heart—the one that inspired her legacy.

We had come full circle.

As I looked down this road, I no longer saw fear, sadness or poverty. I saw joy, and young faces shining with hope. It was a beautiful sight to see: children playing, laughing and singing. Beside them: a health center, ambulance, vegetable garden and school. I saw what

Maddie had seen, what she had envisioned. Now I knew what she knew. These beautiful young children would not be forgotten, nor would Maddie's message. It warmed my heart as I realized the magic I witnessed was inspired by a single act of kindness from *the girl who gave her wish away.*

About the Author

Sharon Babineau, CD, is a decorated military soldier, hockey player, mountain climber, and inspirational keynote speaker. Her most precious role is that of Mother. She is the founder of Maddie's Everlasting Wish a not-for profit charity that was started in her daughter's memory. Sharon delivers inspirational and motivational keynotes and workshops. She is also a trainer and facilitator of several wellness programs for business and organizations: Transformative Mindfulness, Meditation and the 16 Guidelines to Life. She lives with her husband and son, outside of Toronto, Canada.

Sharon has been a guests on shows such as CHCH TV *Morning Show*, CTS TV's *It's All Good News*, CBC's *No Opportunity Wasted* (by Phil Keoghan of *Amazing Race*). She has been recognized for the work she has done at home and in Africa, and is the recipient of many prestigious awards including, most recently, the Queen Elizabeth II Diamond Jubilee Medal.

Sharon is a contributing author of *Chicken Soup for the Soul: Family Caregivers*, *Hooked on Hockey* and the bestseller *Embrace Your Authentic Self*. Her blog talk radio show is called *The Power of One*.

A dedicated caregiver to her late husband and young daughter, Sharon learned the spirit within cannot be broken, and shares her wisdom and insight with her audiences. She believes we are all able to making a difference in the world, and that each of us holds that potential. Sharon works tirelessly to inspire others to do the same. Sharon's company Mindbreak.ca embraces this philosophy.

Sharon speaks to audiences around the world. She is a member of the Canadian Association of Professional Speakers (CAPS) and the Global Federation of Speakers. For further information about her presentations to Associations, Conferences, School assemblies or to book her for an upcoming event, contact the author at *sharon@mindbreak. ca* or visit: *www.mindbreak.ca* and *www.maddieswishproject.ca*.

Appendix A

Honors and Fundraising Efforts

Awards

Maddison Babineau was the recipient of:

- Build-a-Bear Huggable Hero—Canada
- Hamilton Chamber of Commerce Lifetime Achievement Award (first award posthumously awarded)
- Ontario Junior Citizen of the Year
- Ontario Medal for Youth, Ontario Government

Honors

- The Maddison Babineau Memorial Park at Applegrove Co-Op was opened and dedicated in August 2010 in Hamilton Ontario.
- *Canadian Idol* winner, Brian Melo, wrote a song dedicated to and about Maddie called "Move and Be Moved".
- "Aim for the Heart—Kenya", *No Opportunity Wasted*, by Phil Keoghan (*Amazing Race*), aired November 2007 on CBC.
- Maddie named "Most Inspiring Person 2010" —Beliefnet — Editor's Choice
- YMCA Peace Medal 2010, awarded to the M.A.D. 4 MADDIE Student Committee, St. Thomas More High School
- Graeme Newbigging wrote a song about Maddie called *She Lived*

Past and Ongoing Charities and Fundraising Events

- M.A.D. B4 GRAD Initiative (Making a Difference Before Graduating). In Maddie's memory, over 800 random acts of kindness were performed by high school seniors prior to graduating from high school.

- M.A.D. 4 MADDIE, an annual 5K fun run/walk event held across Canada, from Prince Edward Island to Victoria, British Columbia. Started 2008.
- M.A.D. 4 Maddie Dinner Dance and Silent Auction. Started 2012.
- Maddison Babineau Scholarship Fund, St. Thomas More High School. Created 2008.
- Maddie's Everlasting Wish became a not-for-profit charity in January 2011. Maddie's legacy continues through the thousands she has inspired!

Appendix B

How You Can Get Involved

These many achievements were not accomplished by Maddie alone. Hundreds of volunteers worked tirelessly to keep her legacy alive, especially the dedicated committee of M.A.D. 4 MADDIE. Without them, we would not have accomplished such amazing results. We will continue to change the world, like Maddie did. It would be an honor if you could join us. No matter where you live, you can be part of this amazing organization, and make a difference. You can share her message, make a donation, perform one random act of kindness before you graduate, or hold a 5K run run/walk in your community.

To learn how to help, visit: *www.maddieswishproject.com*. Watch Maddie's video at: *www.mindbreak.ca*

Make a wish and inspire the world!

Other Books by
Bettie Youngs Book Publishers

On Toby's Terms

Charmaine Hammond

On Toby's Terms is an endearing story of a beguiling creature who teaches his owners that, despite their trying to teach him how to be the dog they want, he is the one to lay out the terms of being the dog he needs to be. This insight would change their lives forever.

"Simply a beautiful book about life, love, and purpose."
    —Jack Canfield, compiler, *Chicken Soup for the Soul* **series**

"In a perfect world, every dog would have a home and every home would have a dog like Toby!"   **—Nina Siemaszko, actress,** *The West Wing*

"This is a captivating, heartwarming story and we are very excited about bringing it to film."   **—Steve Hudis, Producer**

ISBN: 978-0-9843081-4-9 • ePub: 978-1-936332-15-1 • $15.95

The Maybelline Story

And the Spirited Family Dynasty Behind It

Sharrie Williams

Throughout the twentieth century, Maybelline inflated, collapsed, endured, and thrived in tandem with the nation's upheavals. Williams, to avoid unwanted scrutiny of his private life, cloistered himself behind the gates of his Rudolph Valentino Villa and ran his empire from a distance. This never before told story celebrates the life of a man whose vision rocketed him to success along with the woman held in his orbit: his brother's wife, Evelyn Boecher—who became his lifelong fascination and muse. A fascinating and inspiring story, a tale both epic and intimate, alive with the clash, the hustle, the music, and dance of American enterprise.

"A richly told story of a forty-year, white-hot love triangle that fans the flames of a major worldwide conglomerate."

—Neil Shulman, Associate Producer, *Doc Hollywood*

"Salacious! Engrossing! There are certain stories, so dramatic, so sordid, that they seem positively destined for film; this is one of them."   *—New York Post*

ISBN: 978-0-9843081-1-8 • ePub: 978-1-936332-17-15 • $18.95

It Started with Dracula

The Count, My Mother, and Me

Jane Congdon

The terrifying legend of Count Dracula silently skulking through the Transylvania night may have terrified generations of filmgoers, but the tall, elegant vampire captivated and electrified a young Jane Congdon, igniting a dream to one day see his mysterious land of ancient castles and misty hollows. Four decades later she finally takes her long-awaited trip—never dreaming that it would unearth decades-buried memories, and trigger a life-changing inner journey.

A memoir full of surprises, Jane's story is one of hope, love—and second chances.

"Unfinished business can surface when we least expect it. *It Started with Dracula* is the inspiring story of two parallel journeys: one a carefully planned vacation and the other an astonishing and unexpected detour in healing a wounded heart."
—Charles Whitfield, MD, bestselling author of *Healing the Child Within*

"An elegantly written and cleverly told story. An electrifying read."
—Diane Bruno, CISION Media

ISBN: 978-1-936332-10-6 • ePub: 978-1-936332-11-3 • $15.95

The Rebirth of Suzzan Blac

Suzzan Blac

A horrific upbringing and then abduction into the sex slave industry would all but kill Suzzan's spirit to live. But a happy marriage and two children brought love—and forty-two stunning paintings, art so raw that it initially frightened even the artist. "I hid the pieces for 15 years," says Suzzan, "but just as with the secrets in this book, I am slowing sneaking them out, one by one by one." Now a renowned artist, her work is exhibited world-wide.

A story of inspiration, truth and victory.

"A solid memoir about a life reconstructed. Chilling, thrilling, and thought provoking."
—Pearry Teo, Producer, *The Gene Generation*

ISBN: 978-1-936332-22-9 • ePub: 978-1-936332-23-6 • $16.95

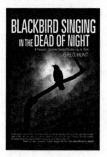

Blackbird Singing in the Dead of Night

What to Do When God Won't Answer

Gregory L. Hunt

Pastor Greg Hunt had devoted nearly thirty years to congregational ministry, helping people experience God and find their way in life. Then came his own crisis of faith and calling. While turning to God for guidance, he finds nothing. Neither his education nor his religious involvements could prepare him for the disorienting impact of the experience.

Alarmed, he tries an experiment. The result is startling—and changes his life entirely.

"In this most beautiful memoir, Greg Hunt invites us into an unsettling time in his life, exposes the fault lines of his faith, and describes the path he walked into and out of the dark. Thanks to the trail markers he leaves along the way, he makes it easier for us to find our way, too."

> **—Susan M. Heim, co-author,** *Chicken Soup for the Soul,*
> *Devotional Stories for Women*

"Compelling. If you have ever longed to hear God whispering a love song into your life, read this book."

> **—Gary Chapman,** *NY Times* **bestselling author,** *The Love Languages of God*

ISBN: 978-1-936332-07-6 • ePub: 978-1-936332-18-2 • $15.95

DON CARINA

WWII Mafia Heroine

Ron Russell

A father's death in Southern Italy in the 1930s—a place where women who can read are considered unfit for marriage—thrusts seventeen-year-old Carina into servitude as a "black widow," a legal head of the household who cares for her twelve siblings. A scandal forces her into a marriage to Russo, the "Prince of Naples."

By cunning force, Carina seizes control of Russo's organization and disguising herself as a man, controls the most powerful of Mafia groups for nearly a decade. Discovery is inevitable: Interpol has been watching. Nevertheless, Carina survives to tell her children her stunning story of strength and survival.

"A woman as the head of the Mafia! This exciting book blends history, intrigue and power into one delicious epic adventure that you will not want to put down!"

> **—Linda Gray, Actress,** *Dallas*

ISBN: 978-0-9843081-9-4 • ePub: 978-1-936332-49-6 • $15.95

Living with Multiple Personalities

The Christine Ducommun Story

Christine Ducommun

Christine Ducommun was a happily married wife and mother of two, when—after moving back into her childhood home—she began to experience panic attacks and a series of bizarre flashbacks. Eventually diagnosed with Dissociative Identity Disorder (DID), Christine's story details an extraordinary twelve-year ordeal unraveling the buried trauma of her past and the daunting path she must take to heal from it.

Therapy helps to identify Christine's personalities and understand how each helped her cope with her childhood, but she'll need to understand their influence on her adult life. Fully reawakened and present, the personalities compete for control of Christine's mind as she bravely struggles to maintain a stable home for her growing children. In the shadows, her life tailspins into unimaginable chaos—bouts of drinking and drug abuse, sexual escapades, theft and fraud—leaving her to believe she may very well be losing the battle for her sanity. Nearing the point of surrender, a breakthrough brings integration.

A brave story of identity, hope, healing and love.

"Reminiscent of the Academy Award-winning *A Beautiful Mind,* this true story will have you on the edge of your seat. Spellbinding!" **—Josh Miller, Producer**

ISBN: 978-0-9843081-5-6 • ePub: 978-1-936332-06-9 • $15.95

Truth Never Dies

William C. Chasey

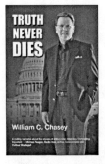

A lobbyist for some 40 years, William C. Chasey represented some of the world's most prestigious business clients and twenty-three foreign governments before the US Congress. His integrity never questioned.

All that changed when Chasey was hired to forge communications between Libya and the US Congress. A trip he took with a US Congressman for discussions with then Libyan leader Muammar Qadhafi forever changed Chasey's life. Upon his return, his bank accounts were frozen, clients and friends had been advised not to take his calls.

Things got worse: the CIA, FBI, IRS, and the Federal Judiciary attempted to coerce him into using his unique Libyan access to participate in a CIA-sponsored assassination plot of the two Libyans indicted for the bombing of Pan Am flight 103. Chasey's refusal to cooperate resulted in the destruction of his reputation, a six-year FBI investigation and sting operation, financial ruin, criminal charges, and incarceration in federal prison.

"A somber tale, a thrilling read." **—Gary Chafetz, author, *The Perfect Villain***

ISBN: 978-1-936332-46-5 • ePub: 978-1-936332-47-2 • $24.95

Out of the Transylvania Night

Aura Imbarus

A Pulitzer-Prize entry

"I'd grown up in the land of Transylvania, homeland to Dracula, Vlad the Impaler, and worse, dictator Nicolae Ceausescu," writes the author. "Under his rule, like vampires, we came to life after sundown, hiding our heirloom jewels and documents deep in the earth." Fleeing to the US to rebuild her life, she discovers a startling truth about straddling two cultures and striking a balance between one's dreams and the sacrifices that allow a sense of "home."

"Aura's courage shows the degree to which we are all willing to live lives centered on freedom, hope, and an authentic sense of self. Truly a love story!"
—Nadia Comaneci, Olympic Champion

"A stunning account of erasing a past, but not an identity."
—Todd Greenfield, 20th Century Fox

ISBN: 978-0-9843081-2-5 • ePub:978-1-936332-20-5 • $14.95

Hostage of Paradox

A Qualmish Disclosure

John Rixey Moore

Few people then or now know about the clandestine war that the CIA ran in Vietnam, using the Green Berets for secret operations throughout Southeast Asia.

This was not the Vietnam War of the newsreels, the body counts, rice paddy footage, and men smoking cigarettes on the sandbag bunkers. This was a shadow directive of deep-penetration interdiction, reconnaissance, and assassination missions conducted by a selected few Special Forces teams, usually consisting of only two Americans and a handful of Chinese mercenaries, called Nungs.

These specialized units deployed quietly from forward operations bases to prowl through agendas that, for security reasons, were seldom completely understood by the men themselves.

Hostage of Paradox is the first-hand account by one of these elite team leaders.

"A compelling story told with extraordinary insight, disconcerting reality, and engaging humor." **—David Hadley, actor, *China Beach***

ISBN: 978-1-936332-37-3 • ePub: 978-1-936332-33-5 • $29.95

Crashers

A Tale of "Cappers" and "Hammers"

Lindy S. Hudis

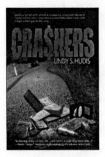

The illegal business of fraudulent car accidents is a multi-million dollar racket, involving unscrupulous medical providers, personal injury attorneys, and the cooperating passengers involved in the accidents. Innocent people are often swept into it. Newly engaged Nathan and Shari, who are swimming in mounting debt, were easy prey: seduced by an offer from a stranger to move from hard times to good times in no time, Shari finds herself the "victim" in a staged auto accident. Shari gets her payday, but breaking free of this dark underworld will take nothing short of a miracle.

"A riveting story of love, life—and limits. A non-stop thrill ride."
—Dennis "Danger" Madalone, stunt coordinator, *Castle*

ISBN: 978-1-936332-27-4 • ePub: 978-1-936332-28-1 • $16.95

A World Torn Asunder

The Life and Triumph of Constantin C. Giurescu

Marina Giurescu, M.D.

Constantin C. Giurescu was Romania's leading historian and author of the seminal *The History of the Romanian People*. His granddaughter's fascinating story of this remarkable man and his family follows their struggles in war-torn Romania from 1900 to the fall of the Soviet Union. An "enlightened" society is dismantled with the 1946 Communist takeover of Romania, and Constantin is confined to the notorious Sighet penitentiary.

Drawing on her grandfather's prison diary (which was put in a glass jar, buried in a yard, then smuggled out of the country by Dr. Paul E. Michelson—who does the FOREWORD for this book), private letters and her own research, Dr. Giurescu writes of the legacy from the turn of the century to the fall of Communism.

We see the rise of modern Romania, the misery of World War I, the blossoming of its culture between the wars, and then the sellout of Eastern Europe to Russia after World War II. In this sweeping account, we see not only its effects socially and culturally, but the triumph in its wake: a man and his people who reclaim better lives for themselves, and in the process, teach us a lesson in endurance, patience, and will—not only to survive, but to thrive.

"The inspirational story of a quiet man and his silent defiance in the face of tyranny."
—Dr. Connie Mariano, author of *The White House Doctor*

ISBN: 978-1-936332-76-2 • ePub: 978-1-936332-77-9 • $21.95

Diary of a Beverly Hills Matchmaker

Marla Martenson

Quick-witted Marla takes her readers for a hilarious romp through her days as an LA matchmaker where looks are everything and money talks. The Cupid of Beverly Hills has introduced countless couples who lived happily ever-after, but for every success story there are hysterically funny dating disasters with high-maintenance, out of touch clients. Marla writes with charm and self-effacement about the universal struggle to love and be loved.

"Martenson's irresistible quick wit will have you rolling on the floor."
—Megan Castran, international YouTube queen

ISBN 978-0-9843081-0-1 • ePub: 978-1-936332-03-8 • $14.95

Trafficking the Good Life

Jennifer Myers

Jennifer Myers had worked long and hard toward a successful career as a dancer in Chicago, but just as her star was rising, she fell in love with the kingpin of a drug trafficking operation. Drawn to his life of luxury, she soon became a vital partner in driving marijuana across the country, making unbelievable sums of easy money that she stacked in shoeboxes and spent like an heiress.

Steeped in moral ambiguity, she sought to cleanse her soul with the guidance of spiritual gurus and New Age prophets—to no avail. Only time in a federal prison made her face up to and understand her choices. It was there, at rock bottom, that she discovered that her real prison was the one she had unwittingly made inside herself and where she could start rebuilding a life of purpose and ethical pursuit.

"A gripping memoir. When the DEA finally knocks on Myers's door, she and the reader both see the moment for what it truly is—not so much an arrest as a rescue."
—Tony D'Souza, author of *Whiteman* and *Mule*

"A stunningly honest exploration of a woman finding her way through a very masculine world . . . and finding her voice by facing the choices she has made."
—Dr. Linda Savage, author of *Reclaiming Goddess Sexuality*

ISBN: 978-1-936332-67-0 • ePub: 978-1-936332-68-7 • $18.95

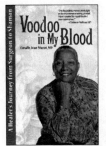

Voodoo in My Blood

A Healer's Journey from Surgeon to Shaman

Carolle Jean-Murat, M.D.

Born and raised in Haiti to a family of healers, US trained physician Carolle Jean-Murat came to be regarded as a world-class surgeon. But her success harbored a secret: in the operating room, she could quickly intuit the root cause of her patient's illness, often times knowing she could help the patient without surgery. Carolle knew that to fellow surgeons, her intuition was best left unmentioned. But when the devastating earthquake hit Haiti and Carolle returned to help, she had to acknowledge the shaman she had become.

"This fascinating memoir sheds light on the importance of asking yourself, 'Have I created for myself the life I've meant to live?'"
> —**Christiane Northrup, M.D., author of the New York Times bestsellers:** *Women's Bodies, Women's Wisdom* **and** *The Wisdom of Menopause*

ISBN: 978-1-936332-05-2 • ePub: 978-1-936332-04-5 • $21.95

Fastest Man in the World

The Tony Volpentest Story

Tony Volpentest

Foreword by Ross Perot

Tony Volpentest, a four-time Paralympic gold medalist and five-time world champion sprinter, is a 2012 nominee for the Olympic Hall of Fame

"This inspiring story is about the thrill of victory to be sure—winning gold—but it is also a reminder about human potential: the willingness to push ourselves beyond the ledge of our own imagination. A powerfully inspirational story."
> —**Charlie Huebner, United States Olympic Committee**

"This is a moving, motivating and inspiring book."
> —**Dan O'Brien, world and Olympic champion decathlete**

"Tony's story shows us that no matter where we start the race, no matter what the obstacles, we all have it within us to reach powerful goals."
> —**Oscar Pistorius, "Blade Runner," double amputee, world record holder in the 100, 200 and 400 meters**

ISBN: 978-1-936332-00-7 • ePub: 978-1-936332-01-4 • $16.95

Amazing Adventures of a Nobody

Leon Logothetis

From the Hit Television Series Aired in 100 Countries!

Tired of his disconnected life and uninspiring job, Leon Logothetis leaves it all behind—job, money, home, even his cell phone—and hits the road with nothing but the clothes on his back and five dollars in his pocket, relying on the kindness of strangers and the serendipity of the open road for his daily keep. Masterful storytelling!

"A gem of a book; endearing, engaging and inspiring."
—Catharine Hamm, Los Angeles Times Travel Editor

"Warm, funny, and entertaining. If you're looking to find meaning in this disconnected world of ours, this book contains many clues."　**—Psychology Today**

ISBN: 978-0-9843081-3-2 • ePub: 978-1-936332-51-9 • $14.95

MR. JOE

Tales from a Haunted Life

Joseph Barnett and Jane Congdon

Do you believe in ghosts? Joseph Barnett didn't, until the winter he was fired from his career job and became a school custodian to make ends meet. The fact that the eighty-five-year-old school where he now worked was built near a cemetery had barely registered with Joe when he was assigned the graveyard shift. But soon, walking the dim halls alone at night, listening to the wind howl outside, Joe was confronted with a series of bizarre and terrifying occurrences.

It wasn't just the ghosts of the graveyard shift that haunted him. Once the child of a distant father and an alcoholic mother, now a man devastated by a failed marriage, fearful of succeeding as a single dad, and challenged by an overwhelming illness, Joe is haunted by his own personal ghosts.

The story of Joseph's challenges and triumphs emerges as an eloquent metaphor of ghosts, past and present, real and emotional, and how a man puts his beliefs about self—and ghosts—to the test.

"Thrilling, thoughtful, elegantly told. So much more than a ghost story."
—Cyrus Webb, CEO, Conversation Book Club

"This is truly inspirational work, a very special book—a gift to any reader."
—Diane Bruno, CISION Media

ISBN: 978-1-936332-78-6 • ePub: 978-1-936332-79-3 • $18.95

The Search For
The Lost Army

The National Geographic and Harvard University Expedition

Gary S. Chafetz

In one of history's greatest ancient disasters, a Persian army of 50,000 soldiers was suffocated by a hurricane-force sandstorm in 525 BC in Egypt's Western Desert. No trace of this conquering army, hauling huge quantities of looted gold and silver, has ever surfaced.

Nearly 25 centuries later on October 6, 1981, Egyptian Military Intelligence, the CIA, and Israel's Mossad secretly orchestrated the assassination of President Anwar Sadat, hoping to prevent Egypt's descent—as had befallen Iran two years before—into the hands of Islamic zealots. Because he had made peace with Israel and therefore had become a marked man in Egypt and the Middle East, Sadat had to be sacrificed to preserve the status quo.

These two distant events become intimately interwoven in the story of Alex Goodman, who defeats impossible obstacles as he leads a Harvard University/ National Geographic Society archaeological expedition into Egypt's Great Sand Sea in search of the Lost Army of Cambyses, the demons that haunt him, and the woman he loves. Based on a true story.

Gary Chafetz, referred to as "one of the ten best journalists of the past twenty-five years," is a former Boston Globe correspondent and was twice nominated for a Pulitzer Prize by the Globe.

ISBN: 978-1-936332-98-4 • ePub: 978-1-936332-99-1 • $21.95

The Tortoise Shell Code

V Frank Asaro

Off the coast of Southern California, the Sea Diva, a tuna boat, sinks. Members of the crew are missing and what happened remains a mystery. Anthony Darren, a renowned and wealthy lawyer at the top of his game, knows the boat's owner and soon becomes involved in the case. As the case goes to trial, a missing crew member is believed to be at fault, but new evidence comes to light and the finger of guilt points in a completely unanticipated direction.

Now Anthony must pull together all his resources to find the truth in what has happened and free a wrongly accused man—as well as untangle himself. Fighting despair, he finds that the recent events have called much larger issues into question. As he struggles to right this terrible wrong, Anthony makes new and enlightening discoveries in his own life-long battle for personal and global justice.

V Frank Asaro is a lawyer, musician, composer, inventor and philosopher. He is also the author of Universal Co-opetition.

ISBN: 978-1-936332-60-1 • ePub: 978-1-936332-61-8 • $24.95

The Morphine Dream

Don Brown with Boston Globe
Pulitzer nominated Gary S. Chafetz

An amazing story of one man's loss and gain, hope, and the revealing of an unexpected calling.

At 36, high-school dropout and a failed semi-professional ballplayer Donald Brown hit bottom when an industrial accident left him immobilized. But Brown had a dream while on a morphine drip after surgery: he imagined himself graduating from Harvard Law School (he was a classmate of Barack Obama) and walking across America. Brown realizes both seemingly unreachable goals, and achieves national recognition as a legal crusader for minority homeowners. An intriguing tale of his long walk—both physical and metaphorical.

A story of perseverance and second chances.

"An incredibly inspirational memoir." —**Alan M. Dershowitz, professor, Harvard Law School**

ISBN: 978-1-936332-25-0 • ePub: 978-1-936332-26-7 • $16.95 US

GPS YOUR BEST LIFE

Charting Your Destination
and Getting There in Style

Charmaine Hammond
and Debra Kasowski

Foreword by Jack Canfield

Obstacles and roadblocks can detour us on the way to success, or even prevent us from getting there at all. GPS Your Best Life helps you determine where you are now, and, through practical strategies and assessments, helps you clarify what you want in your personal and career life, and shows you how to expertly navigate through hidden fears and procrastination so as to get on the road to your best life—now!

A most useful guide to charting and traversing the many options that lay before you.

Charmaine Hammond is the bestselling author of On Toby's Terms, and speaks to audiences around the world. Debra Kasowski is founder and CEO of the Millionaire Woman Club, and a professional speaker.

"A perfect book for servicing your most important vehicle: yourself. No matter where you are in your life, the concepts and direction provided in this book will help you get to a better place. It's a must read."
—**Ken Kragen, author of *Life Is a Contact Sport*, and organizer of *We Are the World*, and *Hands Across America*, and other historic humanitarian events**

ISBN: 978-1-936332-26-7 • ePub: 978-1-936332-41-0 • $16.95

Universal Co-opetition

Nature's Fusion of
Co-operation and Competition

V Frank Asaro

A key ingredient in business success is competition—and cooperation. Too much of one or the other can erode personal and organizational
goals. This book identifies and explains the natural, fundamental law that
unifies the apparently opposing forces of cooperation and competition.

Finding this synthesis point in a variety of situations—from the personal to the organizational—can save our finances, our family, our future, and our world.

V Frank Asaro is a lawyer, musician, composer, inventor and philosopher. He is also the
author of *The Tortoise Shell Code*.

ISBN: 978-1-936332-08-3 • ePub: 978-1-936332-09-0 • $15.95

Electric Living

The Science behind
the Law of Attraction

Kolie Crutcher

Although much has been written about how the Law of Attraction
works, Electric Living: The Science Behind the Law of Attraction, is the
first book to examine why it works—for good or bad. Skeptics and ad-
herents alike will find Kolie Crutcher's exploration of the science behind this this potent law a
fascinating read.

An electrical engineer by training, Crutcher applies his in-depth knowledge of electrical engineering principles and practical engineering experience detailing the scientific explanation of why
human beings become what they think. A practical, step-by-step guide to help you harness your
thoughts and emotions so that the Law of Attraction will benefit you.

"Electric Living: The Science Behind the Law of Attraction is the real deal when it comes
to the Law of Attraction. Kolie's philosophy of Consciousness Creates is the key that un-
locks the door to tremendous wealth. This book is a must-read for anyone who wants to be
successful in his or her personal or professional life."

—**Freeway Ricky Ross**

ISBN: 978-1-936332-58-8 • ePub: 978-1-936332-59-5 6 x 9 • $16.95

Bettie Youngs Books

We specialize in MEMOIRS

. . . books that celebrate

fascinating people and

remarkable journeys

In bookstores everywhere, online, Espresso,
or from the publisher, Bettie Youngs Books
VISIT OUR WEBSITE AT
www.BettieYoungsBooks.com
To contact:
info@BettieYoungsBooks.com

CPSIA information can be obtained at www.ICGtesting.com
Printed in the USA
LVOW100452011212

309563LV00002B/81/P